HOUNDED BY GOD:

A Gay Man's Journey to Self-Acceptance, Love, and Relationship

Joseph Gentilini

Edited by David Schimmel

DESIGN OF COVER

The design of this cover comes from a journal entry the author made in 1984 in which he had two centering images of wholeness. One was the Eucharistic Host and the other a Christian Cross. The rainbow-colored robe over the Cross was added to signify the acceptance of the author's gay identity. These images bring together all of his finished and unfinished struggles and conflicts, and in them the author found his integration.

The design was drawn by artist Michael Dickinson. His website is: info@artistmichaeldickinson.com

First published by Dog Ear Publishing
4010 W. 86th Street, Ste H
Indianapolis, IN 46268
www.dogearpublishing.net

ISBN: 978-1-4575-1961-1

This book is printed on acid-free paper.

Printed in the United States of America

St. Augustine put it beautifully into words: "You made us for yourself, Oh Lord, and our hearts will never rest until they rest in you." Most of us go through life covering over that yearning at the heart of every human, distracting ourselves with the desires of this world. Not so, Joseph Gentilini. God gave Joseph an extraordinary awareness of that call to union with God.

In his autobiographical journal, Joe spells out his painful journey as an active gay man, from revolt against that voice of God to final acceptance with God's grace of his gay identity given to him by God—a remarkable journey which brings hope to all of us that God's call to union is to the authentic self. God dwells within us, and the only way to union with that God is through the authentic self!

John McNeill, former Jesuit priest and author of
The Church and the Homosexual; *Taking a Chance on God*;
Freedom, Glorious Freedom;
and *My Spiritual Journey: Both Feet Planted in Midair*

Anyone who has had their sexuality shamed by their religious tradition should relate to Joe's story of staying connected to his Catholicism while rejecting the teaching of Catholic Bishops on homosexuality and replacing it with a truly authentic spiritual connection with his Creator. He gives the reader access to his most intimate thoughts, fears, and experiences—all of which provide the fuel for a seminal work in LGBT spirituality.

Mark Matson, former president of DignityUSA

HOUNDED BY GOD:

A Gay Man's Journey to Self-Acceptance, Love, and Relationship

Hound of Heaven

Francis Thompson

(1859–1907)

I fled Him, down the nights and down the days:
I fled Him, down the arches of the years;
I fled Him, down the labyrinthine ways
Of my own mind; and in the midst of tears
I hid from Him, and under running laughter.

…Is my gloom, after all,
Shade of His hand, outstretched caressingly?
"Ah, fondest, blindest, weakest,
I am He Whom thou seekest!
Thou dravest love from thee, who dravest Me.

CONTENTS

FOREWORD

I have not peeked into Joseph Gentilini's life; I have stared at it. As editor of Joe's writing, I have read and reread over 5,000 typewritten single-spaced pages of his journal and unpublished autobiography. Tentatively begun in 1966 as a collection of significant cards and letters received, his journal of self-reflective entries began four years later during his final year in college. Retirement from work in 2003 only fanned the flames of what Joe experiences as a "drive to give flesh to my insides."

He has desired to tell his personal story ever since he wrote his 1992 autobiography, which passed through several publishers' hands but only resulted in the depletion of cash and a dream deferred. Through the horror of gay reparative therapy, a conflictual relationship not only with his parents but also his Catholic faith, and oppressive feelings of inadequacy, Joe emerged into acceptance of a gay Catholic identity, reconciliation with his parents, and a committed relationship with Leo Radel. He wanted to show that a person who was so angry with himself, other people, and God could ultimately find his vocation, which is to live the truth of his life as a gay man in relationship with his partner and his God. "It is the journey to myself and to God, even in the midst of feeling lost. This book could be for gays and for straight people—for those who go through hell to get to heaven."

Yet, in 1992, at 44 years of age, his life story was in its adolescence. Joe was a bundle of contradictions—strong and frightened, competent and unsure of himself, sexually tender and aggressive, idealistic and practical, and wishing for a monastic vocation but living a secular one. Loving and generous, he struggled to navigate relationships with his parents, friends, coworkers, and with the man he loves. Twenty additional years have not provided resolution for his complicated humanity, but rather further exploration, perspective, and wisdom.

On balance, Joe's story is probably no more heartbreaking or heartwarming than any other, yet he is continuing to record and contemplate his unfolding consciousness. Reflecting on a journal entry seven years previous, he picked up on a comment about his gentleness and wrote that this is "what my last name really means. *Gentilini* is the superlative of *gentle* as in *extremely gentle and precious*...I want to acknowledge this and allow my subconscious and my conscious mind to integrate it into my personality."

Perhaps this sensitized him to the divine attribute of gentleness. Reading a gospel passage that portrays Jesus as the fulfillment of Isaiah's prophecy, Joe reflected on the words "he will not break a bruised reed or quench a smoldering wick until he brings justice to victory" (Matthew 12:20). Then in his journal he wrote, "Those persons who struggle to discover and do God's will; those persons who struggle with their faith; those searching for God in all the wrong places; those gays and lesbians who are trying to breathe under the weight of the Church's oppression will be dealt with gently. With even a spark of faith and desire, God will be gentle and careful; he will blow gently on the small flame of the wick so that he will not blow it out. He will gently blow on it to keep it lit. He blows gently with me."

Joe personally senses God's gentleness through the concern of people, most especially his spiritual companion, a contemplative nun. Above all, she offers a safe place for Joe to share his experience, listens nonjudgmentally, and asks confounding questions. Still, her wisdom may not have unfolded as fully in Joe's being without Leo's unconditional love. Joe is blessed to have a life partner whose active listening not only grounds him but also sends him back to his journal to name, explore, and embrace the person whom God created him to be.

And so this story of gentleness remains in journal format. Unlike a linear approach, there is no clear progression from beginning to middle to end. Journal writing is not concerned with an ordered flow of thoughts or final conclusions. Rather, it honors the stirrings of the present moment, which sometimes occasions mining the depths of previous experiences or raising yet unanswerable questions. Thus, the journal entries compiled for this book are not always chronological and are unable to bring Joe's life story to completion. On several levels, Joe remains "an open book."

Joe asked me to edit his journals because he realized he could not be objective in the process. Indeed, he envisioned choosing only journal entries that focused on his spirituality. Yet it is impossible to understand an individual's spirituality devoid of life experience from which it grows and matures. His tie to parents, his work experience, and surely his tumultuous unfolding as a gay man in a committed relationship not only shaped his spirituality but also tested it.

As editor, I attempted to bypass most journal entries in which Joe sought to explain what was happening to him and chose those that simply showed what was happening. At times, Joe questioned my approach, which seemed too open-ended. Precisely the point, I believe. The only assistance people need for reading this book of Joe's edited journal is the inner wisdom of their self-awareness. They will see what they need to see, be affirmed by what touches their hearts, and be challenged in those still-evolving areas of their lives.

As for me, staring as long as I did into Joe Gentilini's life, my feelings are as complicated as Joe's humanity. At turns I wanted to hug him, slap him, cheer for him, correct him, be patient with him, do it for him, plead with him to see his goodness, and yell at him to stop tying himself up in knots. An engaging story, however, sees to it that my responses morph into questions aimed at my own humanity. I am no longer reading Joe's story; I am contemplating mine.

In 1977, Joe recorded the first time he experienced God talking to him. God said, "Joseph, I love you." Twenty years later, having grown comfortable conversing with God, Joe asked, "What do you want me to do with my life?" God replied, "I want you to love yourself." If it happened to Joe Gentilini, it could happen to you.

David F. Schimmel
Editor
2012

David Schimmel has a MA in Theology and a M.Div. He has spent the past 29 years working in adult spiritual formation as a program director, speaker, writer, retreat director, and spiritual director. For 18 years he wrote and published a monthly, four-page journal entitled, *PASSION, Spirituality from a Gay Perspective.*

His website is www.makingspiritmatter.weebly.com. Contact him at dfschimmel@juno.com.

ACKNOWLEDGMENTS

I want to acknowledge several persons who had an influence on my life and subsequently on this book. They loved me and I loved them, and they helped me to accept myself as a gay Catholic man. Thank you, GB, RC, Fathers BH, NB, and KM, and Sister LW. Several readers offered me their helpful and objective reactions to the presentation of my story. I thank Leo, Mark, Virginia, Irene, and Molly for their time and effort, which contributed to making this book the best it could be.

I first learned of Father John McNeill in 1973 when I read an article about him in the *National Catholic Reporter*. Later, I met him when he came to Dayton to promote his book *The Church and the Homosexual*. I kept in touch with him, and for the past 20 years, he has read my monthly journal entries. John encouraged me to consider sharing my journal with a wider audience, although I did not know how to do this. He persisted, and I finally agreed. Without his encouragement, this book would not exist.

I do not have the words to thank my editor, David Schimmel, for his work. David patiently read every page of my typed journal, discovered themes, and developed a proper format for the chapters. David was able to put the material together in a way I never would have been able to. If I had been left to my own devices, my tome of journal entries would just be gathering dust on the shelf. Thank you, David!

I want to thank my unnamed spiritual companion, a contemplative nun who has listened to me for many years. Sister told me that she simply put a mirror in front of me so that I could see the goodness that God sees when he looks at me. This was often painful because I could see no beauty. Sister showed me how God has graced my life, even in the midst of my struggles and pain. She showed me how much she loves me and how much God loves me as well.

Always there is God in my life, hounding me to accept his love and to grow emotionally and spiritually. God was present even when I was unaware. Now I am aware and publicly acknowledge the God of my life.

And then there is my partner and spouse, Leo, who loves me with an unconditional love. Without him, I truly believe that I would be dead—physically, emotionally, and spiritually. Leo's love has never wavered, whether through the wonderful years or the difficult ones. My dear sweet Leo, to you I owe my life, and to you I dedicate this book. Thank you.

AUTHOR'S NOTE

This book includes journal entries written before the widespread use of inclusive language. I thought of revising these entries, but my editor suggested leaving them as originally written to show that although I was not exempt from male bias, I eventually acknowledged it and tried to be inclusive in my writing.

In a few places, journal entries are modified for clarification. I never wrote my journal with the intention of publishing it, and so I used my own shortcut language. To make the thoughts clearer, my editor made some judicious changes.

Although the journal entries indicate the date on which they were written, the entries, not the dates, tell the story. Where necessary, names and identifying locations were changed or omitted to protect the privacy of individuals. I did not change my partner's name, my parents' names, or my own name.

I am not proud of some of my behaviors mentioned in this book and thought about taking a few of the entries out. My partner wisely recommended against this and told me, "Joe, there is no redemption if there is no fall. God hounded you because you were resisting God's loving presence in your life." How true!

Contact Joseph Gentilini at gio0848@columbus.rr.com.

1

FLESH TO MY INSIDES

My feelings are too much a part of me, and I don't want to let them disappear.
They are good and beautiful and may be my way of involving myself in the
paschal mystery.[1] My writing is also involved in this. It is a must for me.
Writing results from my drive to give flesh to my insides, my participation in
the incarnation of the Cosmic Christ.[2]
May 29, 1976

I took a ride to a park just to be alone and to think. I felt empty, guilty, and hopeless, and so I took my pad and pencil along to write. I had begun to put my feelings and thoughts on paper the summer before, and it was a way to release tension and put "everything" out in front of me.

Unpublished Autobiography

A friend mentioned today that I look to an impersonal device by writing to release my tension, whereas he searches for another to listen to him. First of all, I do my share of talking to work things out, and in the second place, my writing is not impersonal. In my view, I am talking to myself, getting in touch with my soul and at the very same time communing with my God, who lives in me and abides in me. I live in him. At my core I am with God. If that is true, then at the same time, I am in touch with all others—all men and women—for at their very core, they also abide with God and he lives and breathes in them. My writings are not really impersonal at all. [Writing] becomes a vehicle for me to touch others, myself, and God. It is a sacred thing to do.

June 13, 1976

I feel so good about starting this journal again. I feel like I'm creating something and it is tangible. I know this is going to probably sound arrogant, but somehow, my writing is important not just for me but also for others. I guess I really think that [my writings] will outlast me and people will read them after I'm gone. Maybe that is just my way of saying to others as I did to my mother years ago, "Before you condemn me, read me, read my thoughts and feelings that I don't share with you verbally. Read my prayers, which you don't see or hear because you just condemn me for actions that are wrong in your eyes."

June 16, 1976

Tonight I am aware of my aloneness. I can't say it is intolerable or I'd do something about it. I'd be at the bar or the baths.[3] No, I sit here listening to music, having a drink, reading, and also [being] aware of myself, my okayness. Intertwined with that is also my awareness of God or maybe just my awareness of my desire for him, awareness of my void. Funny, now that I have written that, I feel more settled, more relaxed.

April 15, 1977

I had just begun a new book in my handwritten journals. I added this note: I hope and pray the material presented here will reflect continued growth as a person and as a Christian. I hope the pain and suffering will also give way to salvation and resurrection.

December 13, 1985

Well, it has been a long time since I have written in the journal, and I find myself not wanting to do it now, either. I don't know why, exactly, and wonder if I am avoiding something. I'll try to put some things down here.

December 23, 1990

Here it is, 1992, and while I have things to put in this journal, I find myself not wanting to right now. But I know that I often begin these journal entries with the same song: "I don't want to write" or "I don't want to write much." Why do I, then? Interesting question, and I don't know if I have an adequate answer.

I think that [my journal entries] contain important insights into my spirituality, my belief systems, my religious feelings, my world of gayness, and my relationships. Somehow it is important for me to put down my thoughts, to objectify them. Okay, that being said, now what? Well, I want to dedicate this journal entry, the first one of 1992, to my Father in heaven.

Father dear,
bless my efforts here to write down who I am before you,
even though there will be stories of hatred and sin and impurity and depression.
There will also be, I am sure, stories of hope and courage and inspiration and
love.
Take me, and all those whom I shall write about here, and bless us all.
Bring us close to you where we will be close to each other too.
Help us to love you more and more each day and to reflect you
as you are—pure mercy and love.
Amen

January 3, 1992

This week, while driving in the car, I thought about the conversations I've had with God in my life. They have always been so supportive and loving and encouraging, but I wonder if I've ever really taken the time to believe them. The reason I think I'm wondering this is that I have been reading my old journal entries. There, I'll read my conversations with God, or my own thoughts about myself and God, and they are positive. If I would really believe them, I would probably love myself more and give myself more credit. In some ways, however, I think that this is happening to me already. I am more accepting of myself as Joe, as a gay man, as a man in relationship with Leo.

December 29, 1998

I have read my journals over the years, and I must admit, even to myself, that there is grace in these pages. They show my spirituality—my relationship with God—and it is true that I have tried to the best of my ability to have an intimate relationship with God. Even though it sounds arrogant, it is true that I do have a relationship with God. I do believe that he is very much involved in my life. My spirituality is not false or phony but quite real and true. I am beginning to accept this as true in my life.

December 12, 2000

Going through my journals up to 1986, I am in awe at the growth I am able to see in my integration of my sexuality and spirituality, in my letting Leo into my life and how it has changed because of that. This is not my doing but the grace of God. Yes, I know that I had to cooperate with grace, but I could never have initiated all of this. This is pure gift.

February 28, 2001

I can't imagine giving up my journaling totally, as it is such an integral part of my life now. I think of some people who exercise regularly and they have told me that when they don't exercise, they don't feel as well. I almost feel that way about journaling, although I don't do it or feel the need to do it every day. I don't see how I can quit journaling. It really is part of my prayer life.

October 31, 2005

Keeping this journal for some 35 years, staying in therapy, and keeping in touch with loving priests, nuns, and close friends have enabled me to listen to my inner self. Most of my external work—my job, my educational achievements—has provided me with an income so that I could take the leisure time to look within.

December 27, 2006

I do believe that my keeping a journal all of these years has helped to heal me; it has been and is a catharsis. It is a good thing.

February 17, 2007

I know that it is important to write my journals, to document in some way how God has graced my life and saved me. I guess I can see how it is part of my "gay vocation." My journals show how lost I was once, suicidal and despairing of God, and how God's hand reached down and saved me, brought me out of the pits of New York City and Columbus haunts and gently led me to Leo and to himself.

November 16, 2007

How else can I come to God but as myself? How can I expect that I can ever be holy by living a lie or by being in denial of my true self? Now who is this person and how do I discover my true self? Well, my journal entries have shown that this journey to my deepest core was painful. This journey didn't just mean that I would discover and ultimately accept my homosexuality as a core aspect of my personality, of my very life; it also meant that I would discover God in my homosexuality. It meant that I would discover that God loves me as I am with an intense and all-encompassing love and acceptance and that all God really asked is that one, I love him; two, that I love myself; and three, that I love others as myself.

January 4, 2008

I have never done a focused retreat based on St. Ignatius's *Spiritual Exercises*, but maybe I have done so by accident. Because I have often written in these journal pages how God has touched my life—called me to himself in my youth, followed me as I struggled in my dark night of confusion regarding my sexuality, my paths of anonymous sex in all the wrong places, and my pain from the Church's refusal to understand homosexuality as anything but sin and degradation. He heard my cry to him not to lose me, held me when Mom had so much trouble holding me emotionally, and led me to priests and my spiritual director, among others, and ultimately to Leo. Through the years, God has touched me in such a way that I know he loves me intensely with a love and acceptance that I can't even comprehend.

January 4, 2008

"And Mary kept all these things, reflecting on them in her heart" (Luke 2:19). This is so contemplative[4] and the core of the different Christian paths and spiritualities to God. I think my journaling over these past almost four decades has shown that I have reflected on what my life is about and how I can understand my struggles, pains, and joys. For the most part, I think I have been able to find some meaning in these life experiences in the light of God in my life. This has not happened without pain and suffering. I think it has come about, however, because I have reflected on my own "well" as St. Bernard talked about. In spite of the negative messages I've received from the Church hierarchy and society about my being gay, I have found some "gold" in being gay. I have found a way to unite myself with Jesus's Cross, and there, everything makes sense. None of this would have come about without keeping "all these things, reflecting on them in (my) heart."

January 1, 2009

A week or so ago, I printed out some of my Eucharistic, Cross, and "Shadow" journal entries and have read them over and over again. When I ask myself why I read them over so many times, I don't know the answer. I do know that they are only some of my prayers and reflections over the years beginning in 1971. I remember what was happening when I wrote them, and I repeat the prayers. They show me the difficulty I had in my life to trust my own experiences and to trust God in my life. Trust was not easy for me, as these selected journal entries show, but [the entries] also show that I grew to trust my experiences, myself as gay, and to trust that God loves me and protects me. Even today, I've read them a few times and sometimes just stop and tell God that I want him in my life for all eternity. These journals just lead me to prayer.

May 15, 2009

1. Paschal mystery refers to the suffering, death, and resurrection of Jesus Christ.
2. Contemporary cosmologies posit a continually expanding universe in which everything is interrelated. In Christian terms, the Cosmic Christ is the center of this mysterious energy and those united with Christ are conscious that their beings either collaborate with or obstruct the reality of unity in diversity.
3. The baths (or the bathhouse) was a place where gay men could go to associate with other gay men socially and sexually. As I became aware of my homosexuality, it was the only place I felt safe having sex. Most are closed now because of the AIDS epidemic.
4. Contemplative, used as an adjective refers to a form of meditation; used as a noun, it indicates a person in union with the divine.

THE VERY BEST THAT THEY COULD

Father,
thank you for my parents,
who are very human and who have their faults and pains.
They also did the very best that they could for us children and for me
and I thank you for them.

December 4, 1991

My father is Italian and his relatives came from Northern Italy. My mother is all German and her family is mostly from Bavaria. Both are devout Catholics. I am the youngest of four children. My older brother had a twin, who died at birth. Then my sister; then there is me, the gay one in the family.

March 26, 1979

I remember being very young and taking a nap. Mother had just put me to bed, and she was singing me a lullaby. Her singing always gave me a sense of security and safety. I remember coming home from school in second or third grade and going downstairs, where my mother would be ironing. I'd talk to her about the day and she always sounded interested even though it had to have been pretty boring.

I remember the Halloween nights when Mom would get me dressed up in some homemade costume and I'd go out for candy. I remember the school projects she helped me with, the altar boy surplices she cleaned and ironed, and the school lunches she packed every day for years.

November 10, 1993

In third grade, I remember I was very sick and Dad, you lifted me into your strong arms and carried me to the car, which took me to the hospital. I felt safe in your arms. In 1966, when my brother and I had our terrible car accident, I remember hearing how frightened you were as you drove miles to get to the hospital. I remember the care you both gave me during the months of recovery. I remember how you helped me obtain my PhD by giving me your emotional encouragement and financial support. You were there for me, and I thank you.

May 1, 1989

When I was very young, my father would make things for me. I remember a sword that he made out of wood and I liked it. The memory that I have was breaking it or being angry with it. I think that happened a lot. I would get along with Dad, and yet I knew that not long afterward, I would be angry with him, and I can't remember why.

One memory I have was sitting at the breakfast table around noon. Dad was having the lunch that he liked so well—coffee and bread. I had some too. I wanted to do something that my dad was doing. I think even then I wanted to connect with him; I wanted to be like him in some way.

I remember Dad putting me on his shoulders and walking down the alley behind our house to the grocery store nearby, where he would buy me a toy. That was fun. But I also remember Dad forcing me to ride my bicycle to the Little League ball games because he forced me to play. I was so afraid, and I didn't know how to play the game. The other boys did, and I felt so inadequate. I couldn't figure out why he would do that to me. I had to go alone, and I think that he was ashamed to be with me. He was embarrassed by my lack of interest or ability in sports.

I will never forget the time that my dad, and his brother, came to visit and they were walking up the front steps to go into the house. I was on the swing on the front porch, and I had a doll in my hands. Dad looked at me, and I saw such a look of disgust and distance; I felt so totally unloved and "sick," and yet there was nothing that I could do about it.

I remember coming back to work after getting my PhD in 1982. The office got together a softball team, and I was on it. I knew that I wasn't very good, but they didn't seem to care. I went home to look for a mitt that my brother had years before. Dad was in the basement and asked me what I was looking for. I told him, and he said, "I feel sorry for the team that gets you." I felt hurt and angry, and it brought up so many memories. I just couldn't connect with Dad.

Once I was talking about all the things I had to do for my college BA degree and my job. I was working as a clerk at a bookstore at the time. Dad made a dismissive comment like "You don't know what work is. You haven't worked a day in your life." I felt so dismissed and again, I couldn't ever satisfy him. Nothing I ever did was good enough.

September 21, 1992

Whenever I made a decision while I was growing up, my dear mother would mention all the negative possibilities that "could" happen. Nothing was ever "just okay." Hell, I got that from my father, also. I love my parents, but they were fallible.

April 4, 2009

7

I remember that whenever I wanted to do something on my own or have my dad teach me, he would ultimately do it himself "for me" because I wasn't doing it correctly or he "knew how to do it."

I remember when I was very young and I wanted to go play at St. Mary Magdalene's schoolyard with some of the neighbor kids, Mom said no and told me that we would go together downtown to a movie. I remember another time that there was a kid across the street who had his hand and wrist burned and I played with him and Mom told me that I couldn't play with him anymore. I never could figure out why. Then there was another boy down the street that I was becoming friends with and we were playing one day in the field behind the house. I fell and got dirty and Mom was really upset. As I remember it, whenever I was getting friends or trying to reach out, Mom stopped it.

November 25, 1992

In 1968, my mother and I attended the investiture of my good friend as a Dominican novice.[1] By that time, I was coming out as gay. As I was driving Mom to the church, she told me that she and Dad had prayed about me and my homosexuality, adding that if Dad had a heart attack and died, it would be my fault. Later, in the church, she passed a holy card to me that said that prayer is powerful, and she suggested that I had not prayed enough or even at all.

August 4, 2010

One Sunday afternoon in 1968, I felt so anxious and tense, so confused and disoriented, I got up, left the house, and went looking for sex. I went to an adult movie theater and met a man. We got into his car and drove to a rundown motel on a seldom-traveled road on the other side of the city. I found myself having sex with him, but it wasn't mutual or very satisfying. It had little to do with affection or caring. All I got out of it was the ability to stop the "drive" I felt to touch a man. I was able to calm my inner beast, but I also felt dirty about it. I left with my usual sense of guilt and disgust. There was a difference this time. I felt a need to share my disgust. I think I needed someone to punish me, and so I told my mother where I had been.

She stood there, looked at me, and began to sob. Her shoulders sagged, and the sobs seemed to come from a place in her I wasn't ever aware existed. It was a deep crying I had never witnessed before and have never seen since. I felt helpless, but there was nothing I could do. I felt guilty because I knew that I had caused this pain, and in my frustration, I wondered what I was going to do with myself.

We spoke of it a little later, after she had gotten herself composed. She was repulsed by it and thought that it was a horrible sin, but she tried to be understanding, especially since I was going to a psychologist to be "cured." My mother was sure that her prayers and sacrifices would call down a miracle from heaven and that I would be changed. She believed that all I had to do was to use my willpower, stop the activity, and find a nice girl to marry.

My father found out a few days later, but I could not get through to him. He just could not seem to comprehend it and so refused to look at it. I think it contradicted his image of what a man is really about. Telling my parents and seeing their reaction only made me feel more guilty and worthless.

Unpublished Autobiography

One morning in 1969, I awoke and was lying in bed thinking of all that I was feeling. My mother came to the door to see if I was up or not. She knew that I had been depressed for a long time and that now I was smiling. She asked me why, and in my naïveté, I told her my experience with a priest-confessor who, with a hug, made me feel cared for and loved. What a mistake! She told me that I should be careful of some priests and that the devil works in strange ways. What a bombshell! Here something had happened to me that had filled me up and I wanted to shout it to the world, [and] she wanted to take it and call it sick, dirty, and even diabolical. She took what was beautiful and good and denied it. I felt horrible. She could only see homosexuality in what had occurred between the priest and myself, and she condemned it. For me, she only reinforced the alienation I felt from others and from myself. I was what others hated. I felt terribly alone.

Unpublished Autobiography

The Catholic Times[2]
Friday, October 18, 1974

To the Editor:
  Congratulations on your October 4 article, "Priest Backs Homosexuals' Rights." As a counselor who sees many persons, some of whom are gay, I can only encourage you to continue to discuss such controversial topics. Homosexuals, just as heterosexuals, did not ask for their specific orientation. Regardless of what their God-given nature and psychosexual orientation is, all individuals deserve human dignity, respect, freedom, and civil rights.
  Sincerely, Joseph Gentilini

Little did I know what consequences would result or really what was happening to me. I was again "coming out" in a much bigger way, and while it was liberating, it was very painful to me and my family. My mother's reaction to this letter was to say in hurt, despair, and anger, "I am sorry I ever became pregnant with you."

October 18, 1974

A few days after this letter appeared, I saw my father at his office. After discussing a few nonthreatening topics, my father spoke to me directly. "Joe, I've got to know that you're not like those people you write about. Tell me that you're not like that." His whole tone begged me to reassure him. For the next few seconds, I wondered what to say, and yet I knew what I had to say. I could have lied to him, but only at a cost to my own integrity.

"Dad, I can't tell you that, because I am," I said as gently as I could. His eyes welled with tears that softly ran down his face. My father dealt with the subject much better than my mother. He told me that if that was who I was, then that was who I was. He still loved me but hoped that I would change.

I tried to let him see that being gay was not a bad thing for me but a good thing. I tried to let him see that coming to accept myself—as I am—was an act of truth for me. I could not make him understand, though, and he ended with the comment "I've got to believe that you're going to change. If that is sticking my head in the sand, please let me do it." I assured him that I would not be changing. I had arrived at my own peace and had found that my insides were good. If he did not see it that way, there was nothing I could do about it, and yet it still hurt. I wanted my parents to be happy for me and with me, and they weren't able to.

Unpublished Autobiography

I didn't look forward to Christmas this year. I was not spending it with a lover and was more aware of my aloneness. My sister and brother were with their spouses, and going home to my parents' only emphasized my loneliness so much more. The second reason, I suppose, is the fact that there has been so much hurt between my parents and myself. There is so much that we cannot say to each other anymore, so many "worlds" closed to sharing. This comes about because of my lifestyle, my gayness.

I went home, though, and spent about six hours there. My mom fixed a special dinner; my dad tried eagerly to communicate with me. As I was leaving, [Mom] came up and thanked me for coming home. She looked at me and told me that she loved me. I told her the same. She also told me that she "could kick me" but she loved me. My parents love me, and I love them. We are human, all with our pockets of myths, ignorance, fear, and confusion. We are who we are.

Father, take us all in your hands, in your heart, and bring us close to you and to each other.
In you are our destinies and our beings. And yes, I'm glad I went home.

December 26, 1975

Dear Dad,

Since you and I had that conversation in your office in October 1974, our relationship has improved. You may not agree with my lifestyle or values but you have not thrown it up in my face. Since that time, Mother and I have had words many times with hurt on both sides. Mother recently sent me a note telling me it would not come up in our conversation again and that is good. However, years of tension, of feeling uneasy and uncomfortable (on everybody's part) don't go away overnight. After the last episode, I need to stay away for a while.

I wanted to tell you so you know that I don't want our relationship to break, between you and me or between Mother and me. However, I am me and must be independent. I will come home again but for now must give myself time to let my feelings heal. This doesn't mean you can't call or go to lunch, but let's make it on neutral territory, not at the house.

I have written this letter in honesty and in love. Your son, Joe.

March 17, 1976

Spent the evening with Mom. I notice how defensive I am in a generalized way. Any suggestion she makes, I'm looking out for a trap. I'm sorry to say that, but it is the way I feel. I love the woman, though, and I accept the way she is. I accept my feelings, too. How I wish—in a way—Mother had never found out about my gayness, but I don't think I could have been as liberated as I am if I had not told her.

July 29, 1976

My mother and I hit the topic of my homosexuality again tonight, and of course it was negative. I feel rejected, angry, and frustrated. People from Florida were on the television speaking for and against the gay-rights ordinance down there. I said that the rabbi who was speaking, was an SOB as he spoke against my rights. Mom made a comment, I followed, and there we were. I should have kept my mouth in check, but I didn't. I wonder if part of me still wants acceptance from her or maybe is still angry over past flare-ups and so I bring it up or maybe I am still reacting to my anger at persons who still harbor attitudes such as those people on TV and my mother. Maybe it is all three.

Anyway, my mother said she wouldn't hire me or any gay person if we came to her for a job, strictly because we are immoral. That type of self-righteousness and that rejection of me make me angry.

April 10, 1977

I went home Sunday to see my sister and brother-in-law and the kids. I stayed only an hour, most of which was taken up through eating dinner. I was aware I never looked Mom in the eyes. I want no communication with her. As I got ready to leave, she came up, embraced me, kissed me, and told me that she loved me but didn't think I really believed her. She thanked me for coming home. I did not return the embrace, and my body stood more or less unmoved. I matter-of-factly told her I believed she loved me. Then I left.

That conversation has been repeated many, many times in my head over the last two days, and I am beginning to reach some conclusions. For one, I do believe that Mom loves me but her love is different from my interpretation. In a way, I don't even know what she means by it anymore, for it has often seemed so conditional in the past. Second of all, I don't trust her. Even if her love meant total acceptance, I don't think I could believe her.

Thirdly, she still believes all her ideas about gay people and homosexuality, including her ideas on morality and theology. She has a right to those beliefs, but her beliefs make it difficult for me to believe in her love. How often in the past has she spoken of them, telling me she is sorry the day she got pregnant with me, telling me that I am like a rattlesnake around her neck, telling me that she finds it difficult to say she loves me, telling me that gay people are going to hell, that I am going to hell saved maybe only by the prayers and sacrifices of others. Often in the past, she has apologized for saying words "best kept unsaid" but never told me she didn't believe them anymore. So, when she says that she loves me, is she still sorry I was born? Is she still feeling that I am like a rattlesnake around her neck?

Lastly, I guess I don't care anymore. In a way, whether she loves me or not makes little difference in my life. Or, should I say I have mixed feelings? I suppose I must care someplace or I wouldn't be working with it here. However, I don't want to care anymore, and I honestly feel I am caring less.

I feel like a piece of rubber that has been stretched time and again so that the elasticity is no longer operative. I don't respond anymore, that's all. My mind flashes back to about seven years ago. Mom embraced me and said, "I love you, but I could love you so much more if you stopped what you're doing." Of course, she was referring to my homosexual behavior. Her love was conditional then. Do I believe it has changed? No, I don't really. I just don't trust her anymore not to hurt me. Therefore, I won't open myself up to her emotionally again. She doesn't realize that she will not be able to manipulate me like she has in the past. I will not allow her that much influence.

April 19, 1977

Yesterday was Mother's Day. I do love my mother, and I am aware that she loves me. I must let her be true to herself; I must let her have the thoughts and the feelings that she has, for they are hers. My mother is conflicted trying to accept me, to be proud of me while still having difficulty with my gayness. It is okay.

At the same time, I affirm myself. I am me, with my feelings and thoughts, and I accept myself with them. I love my mother. My mother loves me. I'll let it be. I want to love.

May 9, 1977

Forgive me, Father, for my attitude of self-righteousness,
my attitude of superiority.
Let me never compromise my principles or commit an act of genuine self-hate,
but let me never inflict my ideas on another in such a way as to violate love.

May 15, 1977

I went home today for a few minutes. My father talked to me and seemed depressed. He had tears in his eyes as he told me that he didn't think that we were a very close family. I asked him what he wanted. I told him that he really didn't want to know that much about my life. He agreed and noticed that he probably was being inconsistent. I told him that I had shared things with him but not Mother because it bothered her. He told me that it bothered him too and that he couldn't understand it. He told me that I could never be happy being gay. We talked a little about that and social pressures. He said that society was like that and that it would not change. I told him that I couldn't change who I am and I had to live my life as best I could. I told him that I could try to be happy, but he didn't think that it was possible as a gay man. I told him that if I could find a relationship, I think that I would be happier. He didn't think that a relationship would work; in fact, it was even beyond his comprehension. Then when I spoke about the ten percent of the population being gay, my father said that there couldn't be that many. I cited studies, but he couldn't fathom it.

I feel sad that my father feels so unloved and unappreciated. I hugged him and told him that I loved him, but he had some difficulty accepting the hug. He has closed off many worlds between us and yet wonders what is wrong. I wish that I could break through it. I will try to be more aware of his feelings and try to spend more time with my parents.

December 21, 1978

In 1978, I had written a "Letter to the Editor" in response to an article in the *Columbus Dispatch*. I don't remember the article or what I said in my letter. I had not come out as gay in my letter, but I'm sure one could surmise as much. Anyway, one of the drawers in my dresser had broken, and I had asked Dad to come over to the apartment and fix it for me. I can hardly deal with a screwdriver.

As he was fixing the drawer, he said, "Joe, your mother is really upset over your letter. It is not as if we have a name like "Smith." In reality, there were only two listings for "Gentilini" in the phone book: my parents' and mine. I told my father, "I know Mom is upset, but I need to be able to be myself, also. Since you brought it up, why not sit down after you are done and we can talk." So we both got a beer and we sat down to talk.

For the next hour or so, I told Dad what it was like growing up as gay in his family—my confusion over these feelings I had and the fear of admitting them, not only to others but also to myself. Dad asked me, "Why didn't you tell me?" I answered, "Dad, I didn't have any words for what I was feeling, and when I did, I couldn't say them. I didn't want to tell you, 'Dad, I'm a faggot, a queer. Please love me.'" At one point, I looked up, asking my dad if he was bored with what I was saying. His eyes were brimming with tears, and he couldn't say a word; he just nodded no, he was not bored.

I told Dad about going to the library in fifth grade, looking up the word "homosexual," and being scared to death, not only because I was beginning to think that this identified me; not only because I could imagine how others might react to me; but also because I was beginning to suspect how God, as identified by the Catholic Church, might think of me. Of course, I had no other idea of God except the one that I had grown up with. I withdrew in a panic, burying the thought that I could be "one of those." I told Dad that I had become obsessed with fear during those many years, both emotionally and spiritually.

I told him how painful the reparative therapy was that I had been involved in, although I don't think I went into much detail—that would have been too painful for me to tell and too painful for Dad to hear. I told Dad about being suicidal in the late 1960s and the early 1970s and that I had kept the means to kill myself in the top drawer of my dresser when I had lived in a rooming house for a few years before this apartment.

I told my father that Mom believed that I had lost my faith and was living an immoral life but that actually I was the most faithful of all his children. He nodded yes. When our talk was over, we both stood up and embraced each other with a tender, warm, and close hug and cried. My father, holding me in his arms, said, "Joe, you are always my son. I love you, and you are always welcome to come home."

August 16, 2010

Sometimes in the past I have called my father Dad, and I guess I still do. At other times I've called him Sir and he didn't like it. I think he was hurt, and he said, "Don't call me Sir; I am your father." I often refer to Dad as Daddy when I'm speaking to others about him. I suppose I have even used it with him. But others have commented to me, "You still call him Daddy?"

God, our Father, wants us to be sons and daughters, too. He wants the relationship to be tender, close, trusting, and warm. It seems to me that there is a relationship in all this between my dad and God, and the odd thing is that my relationship with Dad was never as close as I wanted it. Since I can't get too close to him, maybe that's why I want to be so close to my Father-God. Maybe that is why it is still so hard to trust God, to really believe that I am acceptable and loved by God.

June 26, 1983

My mother was depressed last week and called. I was also low, and she knew that and wanted to call to see how I was. I was somewhat low because my sister can invite her twice-divorced boyfriend to Mom and Dad's but I can't bring over my partner, Leo. Mom says it is her conscience, but I don't believe that. It is a social embarrassment, and I feel the judgment! I told her it made me angry.

March 3, 1984

My mother and I talked about holidays in the family, and we both agreed that we'd like to cut them out, but I asked that I not be informed of when the family was gathering together, because I wasn't going to be there and I didn't want to hear about it. I told her that I would celebrate birthdays with them alone, or Mother's Day or Father's Day or whatever the occasion was, but not with the family. She talked about this being our "cross," and within Christian and spiritual terms, I can understand that and can agree.

This is probably one of the biggest pains in my life, and I do share it with my Father, with the Compassionate force of the universe. My mother does the same, and maybe in some way and in some fashion, the suffering is salvific. It's really sad for me to put this down, because the family is breaking and it is broken in many ways over the issue and yet there is such intense love between us all.

Into your hands, Father, I place myself with my life,
and I place my family and theirs.
Love us, and bring us to you and to each other. Amen.

February 8, 1985

I found a small piece of paper under the statue of St. Joseph in my parents' home several years ago. On it my mother had written, "St. Joseph, save Joe. Please!!!" Mom was really tortured over my lifestyle. God, what pain she must have suffered.

February 18, 1995

It has always been painful for me to realize that my parents cannot truly and unconditionally accept me as I am—a man who is also gay. They can accept [my] brown eyes and hair, my hyperness, my sensitive nature, my lack of interest in sports, my absolute [lack of] mechanical abilities, but not my gayness. Unfortunately for them, and to that extent for me, it is as much a part of me as any of the above, maybe more than some.

Since Leo came into my life, I saw some hope for changing viewpoints: My mom went into therapy for a while, Leo was here and could not be ignored, and "goodness ultimately triumphs." Well—it didn't work. My mother's therapist moved and [Mom] would not see another. My mother stopped growing, and I even wonder if she stepped back.

My mother's God is a God of judgment, a God whose love for her was conditional, a God who demanded obedience. Oh, she could, would, and has mouthed "mercy," but the bottom line was "obedience." If this is truly her stance, no wonder my mother has been in torment and no wonder she can't heal the split she feels in totally and unconditionally accepting me.

My dad said that they are not going any further than where they are. While he accuses me of insisting on my way, I do feel that there are two sides here: Yes, I can be as dogmatic and judgmental as they, but we are talking about a part of my very personality, not the color of my shirt! He also accused me of killing my mother, and, to be honest, I haven't worked that through yet. I know intellectually that she wasn't well before the recent blowup, but to say I caused her downfall is guilt I will not own.

December 14, 1985

I remember Thanksgiving of 1982 after Leo and I began to live together. We wanted the family at our apartment and we asked Mom and Dad. Mom said that they talked about it and decided that they couldn't do that. I was hurt and angry. Dad and I met. I think it was his idea. We went to a restaurant and got into a booth. The first thing that Dad did was mouth the words "I love you," with his eyes brimming with tears. I was touched, but I think that my emotions were so hurt, I wouldn't allow myself to feel it too much. We talked about the situation at home, and somewhere along the way, I must have said that I thought he understood me a little. I asked him if he knew when I finally felt accepted by him. When he said no, I told him that it was the day I graduated with my PhD from Ohio University. His face registered shock, and I don't think that I could have hurt him any more.

September 21, 1992

It has been difficult enough to accept myself and then to bear also the fact that my biological family, in one sense, cannot accept and freely love me—that is the cross. At first, I envisioned this as two separate crosses, then as the same cross with my mother on one side and me on the other. We each were pierced with separate nails. We could not face each other, and we both knew that my gay orientation is the cross in my life and that her relationship with me is the cross in her life.

In time, the image changed. I saw the same cross, only this time, the nails that bound me to the cross were the same nails which bound my mother to the cross. When she moved and hurt, I moved and hurt, and there was no way to save or rescue ourselves. Again, we could not see each other, and that is fitting too, because we both have difficulty seeing each other's view on the subject. Or, if we do see the other's view, it has not, so far, enabled us to relieve the pain.

My mother and I are bonded to each other and to the same cross. Somehow, there has to be a solution—interesting, as I write that it may be that there is no solution and that is *the* solution. As humans, we cannot solve the riddle, but in God—the force of total love—the cross is destroyed. In him, the nails are removed somehow.

July 19, 1986

A month or so ago, my mother gave me a copy of the local morning paper's announcement of my birth 38 years ago. I sometimes wonder whether or not she is really glad I'm around. My gayness has caused my parents so much pain (and me, too, for that matter). I suppose she is [glad], but I'm sure she is torn. I pray every day for reconciliation in my family, but I doubt it will come in this life. I do believe, however, that reconciliation is in the Father's hands.

September 1986

Mom and Dad,

For any of my actions or non-actions, for any of my attitudes expressed or unexpressed that have caused you pain and anguish, I am truly sorry. For any of your actions or non-actions, for any of your attitudes expressed or unexpressed that have caused me pain and anguish, I truly forgive you.

Love, Joe

Early December 1986

My mother sent me a card this year for my name's day, the Feast of St. Joseph. She loves me very much, and I do her. It still grieves me that Mother has never been able to affirm me as gay or to accept Leo as good in my life. That is still painful, and yet it is okay, too. I am letting go of my need for her approval. She doesn't have to approve to make it okay for me to be me. She has to follow her own light just as I have to follow mine. Love has transcended the conflict; we have both grown over the years. The conflict will be resolved in Christ, in total love. We are both free.

March 19, 1987

My spiritual director,[3] who is a religious sister,[4] befriended my mother. She and my mother would talk on the phone every Thursday evening. It became an event that my mother looked forward to, although she would not say so to me. My spiritual director kept my mother's confidence and would not tell me the details of their conversations, but she did let me know how much my mother loves me and how much [my mother] loves God.

In June of 1987, my second cousin was in town and my parents wanted to meet for lunch with her. Leo was actually invited to this. Later, my niece graduated from high school and my sister invited Leo to the graduation and reception in her home afterward. She loved Leo, and we both came. My mother told Leo that she really did like him and was glad that he was in my life. She admitted it wasn't him per se that she had difficulty with—it was the moral issue.

18

There were other minor conversations and incidents between my mother and Leo, all of which showed reaching out on both sides. And with my mother's new stance towards Leo and me, my father was freer to do likewise. He treated Leo with no evidence of a problem.

In October, my mother was having a surprise 80th birthday party for Dad, and Leo was invited! She even kissed Leo! And, wonder of wonders, Leo was invited that year to our family Christmas! What a wonderful healing! After this, Leo was considered part of the family and invited to everything. With the help of my spiritual director, my mother broke through her barrier to loving me fully as her gay son.

My prayer has been answered. For years, I have prayed for reconciliation with my family. It is grace, a total gift from God.

March 1988

I'm thankful for the deep religious beliefs and feelings that I have. I thank my parents for helping me to foster them within. These beliefs and feelings certainly are a large aspect of who I am.

September 14, 1988

Leo got a letter from my parents, and so did I. Interesting that they sent us separate letters thanking us for the Christmas celebration and also [for] having them over for New Year's Day. Mom signed the letter to Leo with "Love, Marie and Celso" and mine with "Love, Mom and Dad." I think that they don't know how to sign it if they put the things together since Leo is not their son. This is not a criticism of them. I just find it interesting. They have arrived at an adjustment that they feel comfortable with. I am amazed that they were able to deal with Leo at all, and I truly believe that this is grace in my life. More and more, I am sure that God is in my life, in my relationships, in my career, in my family life. He is always there, loving me and protecting me. What have I done to deserve such treatment? Nothing. I just am loved by a compassionate and merciful God. Thank you.

January 14, 1990

Today is Easter Sunday. Yesterday, the whole family went over to my mother and dad's and fixed their dinner. We celebrated Mom's 79th birthday. She is a frail woman now, and it is amazing and disturbing to see her get old. I don't know how I will cope when she dies, and yet it is Easter and I know that my mother will live forever in the Christ. I will see her again for all eternity.

April 15, 1990

I think that the cross in my images⁵ represents my homosexuality, which is the place of my deepest wound. The cross, in Christian thinking, is the place where our salvation took place, where Jesus surrendered his life, felt pain, was abandoned by the Father, and where we are saved.

In my first image, Mom and I are both nailed to that cross. My homosexuality was abhorrent to me and to Mom, and yet there it was. Mom and I couldn't talk about it; it was a barrier to our communication. In time, the second image appeared, and in this image, the nails [that] nailed us to the cross were the same nails. No matter what either one of us did to try to get off of the cross or to move around, we hurt the other person.

I had always thought that the solution would have something to do with freedom and release—and that is true. In a third image, Mom and I are resurrected from the cross a little. We are separated from the cross, but only by a few inches, and we are no longer in pain. The place of the nails is still imprinted in our bodies, and I suppose that has to be, since I am still gay and the wounds are still there. At the same time, however, as in Christian belief, the cross had become the place of our salvation. I had to accept my homosexuality as a vital and intrinsic part of who I am as Joseph Gentilini. Because I had to accept it (I was pinned to it, wasn't I?), I had to learn to look deep within myself and find out who I am. I had to surrender the images of who I wanted to be and accept the person God made me. Because of this struggle, I went into therapy and became more real as a human being, more congruent, more whole, and possibly more holy. I learned to love my gayness—my cross—because it allowed me to get in touch with myself, my deeper self. It allowed me access to my Eros, the fluids which flow within me, the creative part of me. By accepting me as a gay man, my mother had to transcend her image of who I am and her image of who God is. She had to learn to transcend the God of Law and Judgment and meet the God of Love, Mercy, and Acceptance (I guess I did, too!), and this is also her salvation. We are both freer today, and more whole.

July 30, 1990

On Friday, I let Mom know that I had written a letter to *The Catholic Times* in support of Fr. Richard McBrien, and she got all upset. I told her that the letter was tame. She asked why I had to do that since everyone will come up to her and say something about the letter. She said, "Everybody knows Joe Gentilini." I can't just disappear because I believe as I do and she believes differently.

To the Editor:

Thank you for continuing to print Fr. Richard McBrien's articles in *The Catholic Times*. His articles and insights are like bright sunshine on a cloudy day.

They give hope that the dark days presently in the Catholic Church will brighten. They give hope that the days will end when dedicated thinking theologians are easily silenced, when Catholics United for the Faith[6] are concerned only with rigid obedience to man-made laws, and when the hierarchy seems more concerned with power and control. It can't be soon enough!

Sincerely, Joseph Gentilini

July 29, 1990

I talked with Dad about a lot of things, and then he said, "Your mother is really upset by your letter. The girls that are in Catholics United for the Faith will just talk and talk, and your mother has such a hard time with that. She is very sensitive and takes it very personally." I told Dad that I didn't know that Mom belonged to that group.[7] I told him that I would try to be more careful in the future.

The problem is that I have always felt that I have to be careful about who I am or what I say. Years ago, when I was a senior in college, I grew a mustache and goatee. My parents cried as they tried to talk me into shaving it. I never felt that I could just be me.

August 27, 1990

Well, today I have to acknowledge my insensitivity. Spoke to my spiritual director, and we talked about the letter I sent to *The Catholic Times* and my mother's reaction. How can I legitimately express my concern for what is happening in the Church and fight to change it without opening my mouth and saying something? I don't know, but in this particular instance, I think I could have left out the name of Catholics United for the Faith and also not been so sweeping in my condemnation of the hierarchy. I do tend to make sweeping overall judgments. I was not and am not sensitive enough, maybe. I have to accuse myself of that and will do my best to watch it in the future.

August 31, 1990

Last Sunday, Leo and I went over to my parents' for lunch, and somehow, Mom brought up how her mother used to make these very thin pancakes. I remember them, too. I can still see Grandma at the stove, whipping up these pancakes; they were wonderful. I've never had them since. Anyway, Mom invited Leo and me back this Sunday to see if she could make them. She was really looking forward to it and yet was afraid that it wouldn't work out.

Well, we went today, and my sister and her daughter came too. We all got in the act, and it was really neat to be family together. My mother really enjoyed doing it, and we all enjoyed being there with her. My sister had one skillet for a while and Mom and I had the griddle. It was too heavy for Mom, and even I had some difficulty with it too, but we did it together. On the next batch, Leo had the skillet. It was great for Mom to have us over and to make Grandma's pancakes.

January 28, 1991

Easter Sunday. Mom is really becoming more and more fragile. She weighs only about 104 pounds, and the doctor is concerned. She will be having a series of tests this week to see if there are any thyroid problems again or even cancer. I wonder if I'll have her and/or Dad next Easter.

March 31, 1991

Father, give my parents good years, and when it is time for them to come to you, please let it be a peaceful, quick, and holy death. And help me to handle it well. Thanks, and Amen.

September 6, 1991

My mother is not well. She will probably be gone within a year. This will be Mom's last Christmas. God, how will I ever get along without Mom? The therapist asked tonight what I expect will happen when Mom dies. I have said before that I will be a basket case, but tonight, I said that I would be very sad and will remember all the terrible things that I said to Mom over the years to hurt her. I will remember all the pain that I caused her because of my homosexuality, and I will hurt. Anyway, I told him that I thought that I was the closest to her of all her children and that I was, in reality, her therapist or listening ear for things that bothered her and that didn't concern me. I will miss her terribly.

God, please help my mother come to you.
Let her not suffer too much, and let her death be quick and painless.
God, help my father, too, for he will be very sad.

Leo and my sister have decided that they will take turns preparing dinner for Mom and Dad. They'll make a casserole or something that will last a few days at a time. This should help. Leo got a card from Mom thanking him, but it was really interesting because she signed it "Mom," and that really blew me away. I found it unusual, hopeful, and healing.

November 4, 1991

Dad and I seem to be on a different wavelength now, as if it is an entirely different relationship. Last Saturday, he came over to help me put up the insulation over my balcony door. We got the insulation up rather quickly, and then he came into the kitchen for a piece of pie and a cup of coffee. We sat at the kitchen table and just talked about things. He recounted some of the dreams that he has had lately. They seemed so bizarre to him, with no logic, and we were sitting there laughing about them.

I was watching this from "outside" somewhere and thinking how natural this all felt and yet how strange to me. I have never had that type of relationship with Dad, and we seemed so equal at that moment—like two adults in relationship to each other, neither one above the other. It was so good, and I wanted to tell him that I loved him, but I didn't because whenever I've done that in the past, he [did] not know how to handle it and it [made] him uncomfortable. So we just laughed and enjoyed the moment.

December 4, 1991

My dear mother is dying before my eyes and I can't stop it. She is in pain and I can't do a thing about it. What I can do and what I am doing now is to pray for her.

I offer my mother to you, my Father, to love, protect, and care for her.
Bring her to you, open up your loving arms, and enfold her.
She loves you and has lived her life for you and for her family.
Open your Sacred Heart of pure mercy, Jesus, and bury my mother there,
where she will be safe and joyous for all eternity.
Into your hands, Father, I place my mother and father,
and I beg you to please make sure that I am with them in heaven forever. Amen.

December 6, 1991

Dad was taken to the emergency room. The doctors think that he had a small stroke but can't find anything. It is really unusual for Dad to get sick, and it will be so hard to let my parents go. I wish I could hug Dad, but it embarrasses him and so I only shook his hand when I visited him in the hospital. So formal, but I know that he loves me and I know that he knows that I love him. I'll let it be.

January 14, 1992

Dad was operated on yesterday for prostate and bladder cancer. I picked up my parents yesterday and took them to the hospital. It was important for me to let Dad know that I loved him. While Mom was in the bedroom, I went up to Dad, embraced him, and told him that I loved him. He hugged me back, told me that he loved me, and then said that everything would be all right. He usually won't allow me to hug him, but he did this time.

April 3, 1992

God, it seems that I am facing my parents' mortality, and I'm scared of it.
I don't want to see them suffer in pain and linger,
and yet what control do I have?
Please take them into your merciful arms and bring them home to yourself.
I ask you this in the name of your son, Jesus. Amen.

April 14, 1992

My father, my dear daddy, died into heaven today.

July 8, 1992

Since Dad died, one of the things I'm becoming more and more aware of is my father's humility and goodness. Not that he couldn't be downright cruel at times—he could—but the overall stance of my father, the person underneath the exterior, was humility and goodness.

When I look upon my life, when I had trouble with Mom over my lifestyle or even when I wrote my letters to the newspapers with my name, Dad never condemned me or told me I couldn't. He cried, he listened to me, he urged me to reconcile at least a little. That was also grace and love.

Thank you, Daddy, for your influence in my life. I could never be as close to you as I wanted. You could not be as close to me as maybe you wanted, either, but you did love me, and I think you were proud of me. I need you now, too, to guide me, to take care of Mom, to grow. Please help me.

August 2, 1992

I know that I am close to crying and grieving about Dad. My emotions are right on the surface, and I feel like I'm trying to hold back the waves of grief with my bare hands. I am getting tired of the battle, and I know that I'll lose, but I just don't want to let the feelings out yet.

August 16, 1992

Dad's love for me was there. I just wish I had been able to connect with him better. I wish I had felt more comfortable with Dad. I didn't know

what to say to him so many times, and I'm sure he felt the same void sometimes. Daddy, I did love you, and I still do love you.

September 21, 1992

Yesterday, I ordered flowers for Mom to be delivered today. I haven't
done that for a while and I thought it would be nice for her. The message
I had on her flowers said, "Mom, you are always a source of light and grace
for me. Love, Joe." And it is true. Even in spite of the pain and problems
we have had, Mom is still basically a woman and person of grace and holiness and light for me. She is an inspiration.

January 5, 1993

I just came from Mom's, and she is not well at all. She is having trouble breathing and is disappointed that the operation was not successful. In
fact, she said tonight that she was better right after the operation than she
is now. This makes me suspect that the balloon surgery was only good for
a few weeks. I'm sure the aortic valve is closing up again and pretty soon
she'll be having major breathing problems. I prayed tonight that Dad come
and help her across the bridge. I asked God to please grant my mother the
grace to die in her sleep soon. I don't want to see her struggle.

God, what a grace she is for me, and yet I know that I am also a grace for her.
Thank you, Father, for all the reconciliation that has come.
Truly, we are in your hands.

June 11, 1993

It almost seems to me as if Mom is dying by inches. I told her that I
loved her, and she whispered, "I love you." I said that I didn't want her to
die because I would miss her. Mom said, "I'll miss you, too." I told her that
I was sorry things were taking so long and that she had to suffer this way.
She replied that she really wasn't suffering so much because she can
breathe. I mentioned to her that she would be close to me in another way,
and she said that this was true. I told her not to forget me on the other side,
and she explained with a surprise in her voice, "How can you think I'd forget you? You will be in my thoughts always." Then she added, "It can't be
long now."

October 16, 1993

Dear God, love her into yourself.

October 21, 1993

My dear, sweet mother is dead. I love you into eternity. You are truly at peace now. Welcome into God for all eternity. I want to meet you there someday and only hope that I can.

November 7, 1993

I am at peace with Mom's death. I am sad, but it's a sadness that I can handle. We said all there was to say to each other, and we were reconciled. Oh, what a great grace that was in both of our lives.

December 22, 1993

I think of my family. For all the supposed lack of emotional closeness between us, Dad was more accepting of me than Mother was. And yet, at what cost to him! I know it was difficult accepting me, and frankly, Dad hurt me verbally and emotionally because I was not the man he thought I should be. I didn't spell "man" in the way Dad or society could read.

I picture my Dad coming to me now from heaven, holding me, and saying, "Joe, please forgive me. I did not know how to touch you, to connect with you. I was human and had a hard time with your lack of interest in 'man stuff.' I did love you. Please call on me now, here in heaven; I'll hear you and take care of you. Can we be closer now, son?"

"Yes, Dad, I'll try to be closer. I do forgive you and I also love you. I wish I would have had the chance to say good-bye while you were alive. I always wanted a closer relationship with you but didn't know how to do it, either. Can you forgive me, Dad?"

"Yes." (Sigh)

January 25, 1994

In 1999, I had heard that my mother read an obituary of a man who was the son of a woman she knew. He had died of AIDS. She went to the funeral home and spoke to the woman, who had not been reconciled with her son before his death. She was able to bring peace to that woman. Mom told my spiritual director, "If God could give me the grace, in spite of my stubborn righteousness, I had to be there for that mother." What I didn't know was that she went to the hospital and nursing home for other mothers who were having difficulty with their sons who were dying of AIDS. My spiritual director told me of one story when Mom went to a hospital. The son was dying in the room but the mother was in the hall, refusing to go in and touch her son. My mother sat with her, comforted her, and asked, "If you, his mother, will not go in and touch your son, how will God touch him?" The mother got up and made peace with her son before he died. My mother!

January 21, 2007

*I pray for all those gay and lesbian persons who
still live alienated from their families
because of ignorance, fear, and bigotry.
I pray for all the parents who cannot find it in their hearts to love their children
or who are just torn apart by their inability to transcend the issue and just love.
And I thank you again for all that you have done, do, and will do in my life.
Amen.*

December 23, 1995.

1. A Dominican novice is a person who makes a year-long discernment regarding his/her commitment to a religious community. St. Dominic established the Dominican Order in the early 13th century.
2. *The Catholic Times* is a weekly newspaper of the Catholic Diocese of Columbus, Ohio.
3. A spiritual director is a person who companions people by helping them recognize the presence and action of God in their lives.
4. A religious sister is a woman who has dedicated her life to God as a member of a religious community of women.
5. See previous journal entry on July 19, 1986.
6. Catholics United for the Faith is a lay-sponsored group that believes, promotes, and lives a strict interpretation of the teachings of the Catholic faith.
7. I discovered later that my mother did not belong to this group.

3

COMPASSION AND AN UNDERSTANDING HEART

There is inside me something that wants to believe, maybe knows, that I can be a good counselor and therapist. Also, if I want to use a system of "religious belief," then God's name or word for me is that of compassion and an understanding heart.
February 6, 1978

On this date in 1969, I flew to Maddens Inn and Golf Club in Brainerd, Minnesota, to work for the summer. God, was I scared; scared not only of leaving home for the first time on my own, scared of doing a good job, but also scared of my gay feelings and what to do with them.
May 20, 1991

I am a full-time vocational rehabilitation counselor in the ghetto of Columbus. I am also taking courses at night at The Ohio State University, working toward a master's degree in guidance and counseling.
November 24, 1973

Father, how beautiful people are—really. My client is so afraid.
Here he is, living in the ghetto because he cannot live anywhere else—
he has no money.
He is a self-made man, knowing only one trade. However, Father, he can no
longer work at that trade because of his health. Now he must try something new,
and he is so afraid.
He wouldn't go yesterday to training, but I talked to him
and almost had him convinced.
This morning I stopped to take him, but he would not go—I talked to him,
told him I was proud of him, that I believed in him, that I knew it was hard,
I knew he hurt, but that I also believed he could do it.
He trusted me, and I convinced him to go.

Father, what a combination you have made.
A combination of such frailty and strength.
John is afraid; he is frail, vulnerable, sensitive, and so beautiful.

He needs people to see that he's a man, that just because he's out of work,
just because he can no longer physically do his former life's work, he is still okay.
But how strong.
This morning, with your help working in him, working in that part of him that
wanted to get well, and with your help working in me showing him that he is
good, manly, and beautiful,
he took his first steps in training for a new life's work.
What an obstacle, what a frightening thing, but he did it.

You live in him, Father, and he and I are brothers in Christ.
Help me to help him and touch him with your love. Touch me with your love, too.
Love him, Father, and make him feel it.

February 1, 1972

I got my grades from school the other day, and I got A's. So far in graduate school I have a 4.0 average. I sure hope that I can keep it.

November 24, 1973

At work I was (1) elected by my peers to be on the Council of Counselors, (2) elected by my peers to be a board member of the Central Ohio Rehabilitation Association, (3) appointed by the administrative assistant to be the alternate to the Exceptions Committee, and (4) chosen to be part of a survey that the federal government is conducting. Not a bad record, I think!

May 27, 1976

Today at Goodwill Industries, an instructor, a psychological intern, a client, and I had a contract meeting. After the client left, both the instructor and the intern told me that I handled a difficult situation very well. They congratulated me. I felt that I had done a good job, too. That just increases my desire to be a therapist.

July 19, 1976

My immediate supervisor told a counselor that she wished she had ten counselors like me working for her. Felt good!

November 15, 1976

I was invited to give the graduation speech today at Goodwill Industries. My client was graduating along with five other girls. She completed her nurses-aide training after a long and difficult struggle. After she got her diploma, she told the crowd that I was the most patient person she had ever run into.

December 17, 1976

Tomorrow, I have an interview about a potential teaching job at Columbus Technical Institute. I'm uncertain of myself, and I suppose part of that is normal. However, I feel more than uncertain; I feel inadequate to teach. Even though my intellect forces me to see that I have graduated with a BA in social work and an MA in counseling, I feel ignorant of how and what to teach.

January 12, 1977

Spoke to a psychologist at Columbus Area Mental Health Center today concerning several clients. At the end of the conversation, she gave me a compliment. She told me that she had been on a panel at The Ohio State University in counselor education last week with two other psychologists. At one point, they got talking about community resources. Someone brought up my name in relation to the Bureau of Vocational Rehabilitation. It was mentioned that the maze of red tape is discouraging but that it wasn't so bad if the client got Joe Gentilini for a counselor. They all agreed. It makes me feel good to know other professionals acknowledge and respect me. It makes me feel good that I have such a reputation in the community. It is difficult for me not to minimize the compliments because of my strong feeling of inadequacy. I will try, however, to stop the negative and to enjoy, to accept the facts as given.

February 9, 1978

I feel burdened in a way. I get involved with people's problems and lives. That is draining, but I also get something terribly good from it, too. I grow in my ability or openness to being in an intimate relationship with others. I grow in my capacity to give, to be open. I grow in my awareness of God working in my life. I grow in my awareness of my goodness. I am able to be close to someone, to be vulnerable, to be strong, to be adult, to be child. I grow! And it is good.

July 23, 1978

I continued at my job with the State of Ohio as a vocational rehabilitation counselor until 1978 when I took a leave of absence to go to Ohio University in Athens, Ohio, and work on the PhD in community counseling.

November 8, 1981

I remember two episodes in my doctoral program where it was the fear of not measuring up in front of others that so terrified me. In one case, I was taking a practicum class and had in therapy a client who was extremely effeminate. I was not comfortable with this girlishness at the time and didn't know what to do with him. (I would be far better today.) We had to tape our sessions and then share them with the class and/or the instructor. I remember talking to the instructor about it and feeling bad because I did not do it perfectly. There were places where I could have said X or put the focus on Y and didn't. I must have been very negative on myself, because he said that I had to realize that I was in a doctoral class and we were all doing well, although some were better at this than others and I was not the best.

The other instance I remember was sharing a tape with the practicum class. Some of the others were commenting on it, suggesting this or that, and I remember getting up from the class, walking out, and going to my office to stare out the window. I felt defeated and embarrassed. About ten minutes later, I walked back in and then had to deal with the others being pissed at me for walking out (and rightly so). I felt very inadequate and was sure that others could "see" it.

May 20, 2003

My doctoral graduate work was honored as I was given the Donald Green Award, given by my school to the graduate student of the year, based upon academics and commitment to the career. My advisor told me that one of the reasons I received the award was because of my excellent work on my comprehensive examinations. I wrote more than any student had ever written, a total of 80 typed pages. In addition, during the oral defense, one of my committee members stated that he was quite impressed with the amount of knowledge that was shown in the answers.

I have a lot of personal qualities that others recognize. I have a great deal of warmth, which is shown in my concern for others, especially the downtrodden, the oppressed, the poor, and the underdog. I reach out to those in pain. I have the ability to make others feel at ease or not, depending on my motivations. My personality is able to let others know that they are welcome and that it is safe to open up with me. This is a real asset in working with others professionally and also in my own personal relationships.

Undated 1981

I graduated from Ohio University with the PhD on June 12, 1982.

June 14, 1982

My doctoral dissertation concerned burnout and the Bureau of Vocational Rehabilitation counselors in the State of Ohio.

October 14, 1982

I taught at Columbus Technical Institute after my doctoral years and while I was working at the Bureau of Vocational Rehabilitation. I would ask for a reaction paper every week, and the students could react to anything that was taught. This was one response:

Your Human Behavior classes have been just exactly what I have needed for a very long time now. Since your classes, I have had a whole new world open up to me. I can see things the way they really are now. It was a very painful experience for me because I had to face the hurt, pain, and loneliness that I had locked up tight inside me. I found my strength in my self-awareness, and you have helped me to do this. You are a very good instructor.

And a card from a former client:

Joe, I can never express my appreciation enough for what you have done for me during the past year and a half. Just want you to know that I feel I have been very lucky to have had you working with me and giving me the confidence and help I needed to get through a very rough time in my life. I could never have done it without you. Thanks so much! Forever grateful.

September 11, 1983

I was nominated for two awards in my agency, and this past week, I got notice that I won the highest award given by my agency, the Commissioner's Award. I like it, and yet it still feels odd, almost like a cognitive-dissonance sort of thing. It confronts my self-image and my self-confidence. I wish I acted out of the place in me which others experience or see as so strong and competent. What do I get out of not truly accepting it?

December 13, 1988

Rehabilitation demands that we care about others and encourage them. I don't believe that a person can be effective in this line of work, doing this job, with the mentality that "it's just a job." While I am aware of the danger of burnout and the need to detach and set limits, I also believe that a person must have a certain set of values that say that people are important, that an individual has worth and can achieve and grow.

Rehabilitation is hard work, both for the client and for the counselor, and it takes caring, compassion, and commitment to do it. It is important for us to be able to work with ambiguity and to be as flexible as possible in allowing the client to try things differently, to experiment, to take time in their program to regress, and even to fail. Rehabilitation takes heroism, and I have seen heroic actions performed every day in the offices of the counselors and in rehabilitation facilities.

What we do and what we profess toward the client is something that we all need to do and profess toward each other. We expect employers to be accepting of our clients and to be accommodating. I think that it is important that we do the same for each other. I think that it is important that we care about each other and accommodate each other's idiosyncrasies, personalities, and vulnerabilities, as well as each other's strengths. We need to be sources of encouragement for each other.

Commissioner's Award Luncheon Acceptance Speech, July 20, 1989

I was really surprised by my dad's reaction today. After my speech, my dad had tears in his eyes. His voice broke, and he told me I did a good job and that he was proud of me. He even hugged me. Neat. Then my mother got up, hugged me, and told me that she loved me and was proud of me, too. Thank you.

July 20, 1989

I have been feeling depressed and trapped/anxious. I no longer want to do my job, and I don't agree with the direction of the agency. They want to serve only the most severely disabled individuals, and I don't want to.

March 24, 1990

I am angry because I don't like the new direction of the agency—dealing with persons so mentally retarded and developmentally disabled that their chances of a job in the real world are practically nil. While it may be possible for them to work (and I question this), I don't want to be the one to help them. I would rather help those persons who, with a little help and assistance, have a better chance to contribute to society and to feel better about themselves. This is not the direction of the agency, and I will either have to try to "ride it out" or get out. We will see.

March 26, 1990

I'm losing my passion, doubting my skills and abilities, and burning out. My dissertation was on vocational rehabilitation burnout, and I'm "diagnosed." It is not just the mental health caseload, because, in some way, I deal better with those than with the severely disabled physical cases. It's time to move from casework, period.

June 29, 1990

Last week, the director of the Bureau of Vocational Rehabilitation spent a day with me in the field, and when we met one of my clients, she told him that I was one of her best counselors. Today, when I was in her office, she told me, "I have known you a long time, Joe, and I've always liked you and admired and respected you. There was no reason not to. Since I've worked more closely with you, I admire and respect you more. I want you to listen to me and to hear me." I find it hard to hear, frankly, and I hugged her.

August 21, 1990

I now must admit that I cannot stay at my present job—I am no longer satisfied there and I don't think I can give my clients my best. I have lost or am losing my sensitivity and my caring. In addition, I no longer believe the philosophy of Ohio's interpretation of rehabilitation.

March 23, 1991

Please, God, get me out of the job I've got. I'm losing my mind. Please!

July 1991

Twenty-five years ago this afternoon, my brother and I were in a serious car accident in which we almost died. When I see the clients that come through our office with brain damage and ruined lives, I thank God that I came out without a scratch. I do have something to be thankful for, in fact, many things.

Thank you, Father.

July 23, 1991

I am still at my job at the Bureau of Vocational Rehabilitation and having a hard time. I no longer want to be there; I don't get anything in terms of my spirituality anymore like I used to, and I don't believe in the philosophy that the administration is giving in terms of helping only the most severely disabled. This has created a real dilemma for me.

Please, God, get me out of there into something that will refresh me and allow me to help others. Please?

September 1991

I have four people on my caseload who are at very high risk for suicide, and I find it overwhelming. Tonight I saw a person and I know that I was therapeutic for her. Her self-esteem was so low, and she cried about the mess of her life. I prayed for her silently and told her that I thought I could help her. She said that I am a very kind man. I know that I can help some persons, and maybe that is why I am here.

Father, I offer you my frustrations and sufferings for the reparation of my sins[1]
and those of the whole world.
Please use me and give me some relief on my present job.
Help me to know what to do, please.

December 12, 1991

This weekend, I was in training at a symposium on cognitive therapy.[2] God, I really enjoyed being in the group, listening to the "experts" do their theories and therapies. I am intellectually stimulated by it all, and yet when the role-playing began and the individual actors began to "display" their problems and the therapist was there to help them, I felt some panic and anxiety inside. I would not want to be there, or I felt totally inadequate to help them. I am so conflicted with it all. I felt that I had to "cure" them or have all the answers, and yet I saw some of the experts not have all the answers; they tried what they could, and some, frankly, were better than others. Why can't I ever let myself off the hook?

September 21, 1992

Work has been very stressful for the past several days, and I can feel myself getting all hyper. I've got to let it down and just [not] try to do everything. I am not God; I am Joe Gentilini, a human being.

January 28, 1993

Even while I get better at dealing with my "junk" and in trying to give myself credit for my talents, I still have a great deal of difficulty affirming myself. Today at the spa, I was thinking about this again and decided that if this is my cross, then I'll tell God that I do accept it. I accept my life as it is with all its problems, insecurities, and inadequacy feelings. I also accept my life with my good qualities and my basic goodness in God. If this is my cross, then I accept it.

Please use it, Lord, for my own salvation and for the good of others. Amen.

February 2, 1993

Father, I want to use my life as a reflection of you.
I want my life to be one in which I have not wasted talents
and in which I have struggled well with my crosses.

Enter my life, please, and fill me with your love, mercy, and compassion
toward myself and toward others. Amen.

February 8, 1993

Today at work, I was hyper and I had problem after problem after problem. I can't solve them all. I get frustrated, and yet I don't have to live these lives and I don't have to be the person's parent, teacher, or sibling. I only have to do what I can while I am with them. Is this enough? It has to be. I remember that when I was hyper this morning, I purposely said the Morning Offering[3] and offered it up to Jesus[4] for my salvation and [the salvation] of the world. Maybe a little bit helps.

February 12, 1993

Had a busy day at work today. Even though I am not happy at work,
I thought today, Lord, that you want me to be there for some reason.
If that is so, then help me to do your work there; please give me some peace about
it.
Into your hands, Father, I place my destiny and my being.

March 2, 1993

My boss got a note from a client of mine this week, and [my boss] gave me a copy. It says:

I don't believe we have ever met in person although I'm sure that my name has come across your desk. I am one of Joe Gentilini's clients and I would like to take this opportunity to express my heartfelt thanks to you and Joe and all the folks at Vocational Rehabilitation for turning my life around. I was once without hope and was bitter because of it. Now, I am going to school and learning new skills. I'm getting the help that I so desperately needed, all because someone cared and had faith in me. For this, I thank you! and I pledge to do my best.

March 19, 1993

Glad today is almost over. It has been hectic. Had a session with my boss over my caseload—its low number of clients and closures. She talked about how all caseloads are being looked at from "on high" and that included mine. People high up were having trouble with my caseload because I am a "senior" counselor and should be doing better. I agreed, and I said that I would try but I have no control over how clients get through the system; I have no control over the tragedies of their lives, and I won't own it. I will do what I can do and no more. I certainly will not have a nervous breakdown over it, that's for sure.

July 26, 1993

I had a fellow counselor on Monday come into my office and talk about some personal problems. I went to another level in her awareness and told her where the problem really lies—inside herself and in her self-image. She teared up and said that I was very right. We talked some more, and she said that it really helped her. Yesterday, she told me again how helpful I had been and what a good counselor I am.

December 22, 1993

Please, Lord, help me to use my life here on earth to love—to love myself fully
and not in the way I often do. I often don't give
myself credit for the good that I do,
for the fact that I am intelligent, adequate, and competent.
It is easier for me to shy away from responsibility by listening to my old tapes of
inadequacy and false humility. Help me to love myself sufficiently so that I can
openly, honestly, and without reserve love others.
Help me to be a saint,[5] please. Amen.

January 9, 1994

Spoke to the facilitator of the grief group, which ended last night. She asked me to be a co-facilitator of the group she is starting soon for gay men who have lost a loved one. I will think about that. I felt honored that she asked, surprised that she felt I was "good enough," and interested in the prospect. It would give me some good experience in doing this and maybe open an avenue to me for something new, different, and helpful. I'll think about it.

April 19, 1994

Received this story from a former client about our first meeting and how much it influenced her. She is now working in a personnel office of a local hospital and doing okay. It is a powerful story, however, and I am very humbled by it.

When I first walked into his office, I didn't know what to expect. As a newly recovering alcoholic, I qualified for rehabilitation services, and boy, did I need help. I had been so affected by the disease of alcoholism that my life consisted of support groups and trying to survive. Joe knew that I had gone from being a creature of habit to a creature of crisis.

As I laid out my story for him, he sat quietly listening. He listened to my hopes of becoming financially independent for the first time in my life. I had been a banquet waitress when my husband and I separated. I spiraled downward into alcoholic despair. I got into a recovery program and began the journey back to a sane life. Faced with the dilemma of working around alcohol and trying to recover left me no choice but to quit my job and file for welfare to support my children. I had problems all right, and Joe knew that it would take nothing short of a miracle to help me. I had come to the right place.

I told Joe that I was being evicted from my apartment while waiting for my first welfare check. I ate from food pantries and lived on support group meetings, therapy, and hope. When Joe asked me how I expected to get through any program without going under, I fell apart. It had been a long time since I had a good cry! Joe knew exactly why I was afraid in the face of insurmountable odds.

Joe looked at me across a messy desk and smiled as he picked up the phone. He saw my puzzled look and said, "I have a hotline to heaven." (He was calling an angel?) He talked to "the nuns" and one of the good sisters asked Joe what I needed. Not knowing where to begin on that list, he handed the phone to me without warning and said, "It's an angel for you." I dried my eyes and gathered my wits as best I could before taking the phone. The voice on the other end wanted to know if my landlord would let me stay if she paid my back rent. I cried for relief—in disbelief, almost. I had been getting on my knees every morning for 4 weeks because a counselor had insisted that God was my only hope. After 17 years of drinking and separation from God, could miracles happen for even me?

I am not sure to this day that Joe isn't one of God's angels. I walked out of that office that day with more than I ever bargained for. When I left Joe, I was absolutely convinced that not only was God real, but that miracles do happen! Joe's faith in God had translated into faith in me.

I love you, Joe.

Wow! Can I doubt that God loves me, works in me, and takes care of me? I don't see how in the face of something like the above. He does use me and he has gifted me by letting me know it. If I choose, I can also hear God in her voice saying, "I love you, Joe." Amen.

November 15, 1994

Today, I was at a school, interviewing a consumer and his parents for the Bureau of Vocational Rehabilitation. His teacher was there, as well as the work-study coordinator and the guidance counselor. It was an interesting interview, and when it was over and most of the people had left, the guidance counselor mentioned to me that she enjoys watching me (she has seen me before) because of the way I work with people. Later, the work-study coordinator mentioned that I am good at working with her students and families. She mentioned that she had told the teacher before the meeting that I would catch things that were said and use them. It amazes me every time that someone remarks that I am doing a good job, especially when it involves my counseling skills, because I never think I am a really good counselor in the traditional sense of that word.

March 16, 1995

I applied for two jobs with my agency and got both—one for research and planning and one for human resource/development and training. I lean toward the training one, and then I wonder if I just shouldn't stay where I am. I have never been happier in my job with the Transition Counseling Project, for which I began working in November 1993. Yet would I be able to continue doing this without a caseload? Who knows? There is no guarantee they wouldn't end the contract in a few years. I can't mind-fuck like this. I will make a decision and hope for the best. The fact is, I have prayed about this and have really tried to put it in God's hands, to trust him. I'm not very good at the "trusting thing," but I want to be.

Dear Father, I place myself, my destiny, and my vocational life into your hands.
I place these jobs in your hands, too.
Please help me to do the job where I can be most satisfied and happy,
and also be of value to the agency and to others.
I am counting on you not to let me pick something that will not be good for me.
I am counting on you not to let me pick something that will be a disaster
for my own emotional peace. I ask you this in Jesus's name. Amen.

April 10, 1995

I interviewed for the planning job late yesterday afternoon and the human resources job this morning. I had so many mixed feelings [because] my present job is wonderful but no one knows if it will last. Anyway, I signed up for the Human Resources job this morning, despite all my fears. I've prayed hard that God will guide me in this choice and take care of me, not lose me, not let me lose my sanity over it all, and not do a bad job. Trust is not my strong tendency, and yet here I am, trying to trust God to help me.

Please, Father, don't lose me!

April 14, 1995

On Tuesday, I am saying good-bye to the Transition Counseling Project staff that I've been with for over a year, and then on Wednesday, my office staff is saying good-bye to me. I have worked with some of these persons for 23 years, and I've been in my office for 15. It will not be easy. I still wonder if I made the right decision to leave and go into Central Office. I have prayed about it, though, and I trust that God will take care of it for me and make sure it is okay for me.

Jesus, I trust in you and thank you. Amen.

May 13, 1995

It has been a busy month at work, and I have been working very hard at getting out of my position and moving to Policy and Procedures. I am praying that what the other manager of Policy and Procedures is doing to get her position filled quickly will happen and I can move right over.

October 22, 1995

I did get the job in Policy and Procedure. Thank you, God. Most people don't think I'll like it, but we'll see. I think I will like the environment of the office if nothing else.

January 31, 1996

I am very stressed at work right now and feel totally out of control. I am dealing with legal issues regarding the agency's Informed Choice policy, which is in conflict with our Vehicle Modifications policy. I am the one who is supposed to be doing the policy and making recommendations, and I'm lost. My inadequacy feelings are so high about now that I don't think I can go to the bathroom and do it correctly. All the while, my bosses seem to take it in stride and tell me, "You're doing fine." Well, why the hell don't *I* feel it? I guess it does keep me humble, but it is so painful to know that I am smart with a PhD and feel like a seventh grader. Remarkable.

March 4, 1999

Today I received a phone call from the president-elect of the Ohio Rehabilitation Counseling Association telling me that I had been selected to receive the Citation Award at their spring conference. It is an honor to receive it, and yet it amazes me at the same time. If these people only knew my own sense of inadequacy, but they don't—they see me as accomplishing a great deal. This is part of my own cross, and I accept it.

March 31, 1999

Yesterday afternoon, just as I was getting ready to leave my office, the phone rang. I don't usually answer the phone "after my work time has ended," but this time I did. It was a former client of mine from about six years ago. I have had no contact with him since then. He was an artist, religious with an evangelical fundamentalist bent, and only moderately disabled. He told me that he had never had a chance to thank me for all the help that I gave him over the years. He finished college, got married two years ago, has a child on the way, and is doing fine. He told me that I had helped him so much when I was his counselor. I thanked him for calling me.

February 11, 2000

Last spring, I was invited to the northwest area to help the vocational rehabilitation staff better understand the Informed Choice policy of the agency. It was well received at the time. The area managers of the Bureau of Vocational Rehabilitation were in meetings this week, and I guess they discussed my presentation. Yesterday, as I was leaving the meeting with the Rehabilitation Services Administration auditor, the Bureau of Vocational Rehabilitation director told me that she heard what a wonderful job I had done and all the managers were encouraged to find opportunities to use me. That is nice to hear. It still amazes me that I hear all of these good reports on my work and yet I so often feel inadequate at what I do. Amazing cognitive and emotional dissonance.

July 20, 2000

Today at 3:45 p.m., I reached my thirty years of government service and so can retire with a pension and my health insurance any time I want. This is a nice feeling, although I don't think it has really sunk in yet. Of course, I still plan to work for the state for a year or so—maybe.

April 30, 2001

I was at a meeting today facilitated by one of the commissioners. After the meeting, I told him privately about my retirement. He said that the agency will lose such a wealth of institutional knowledge when I walk out the door, but he congratulated me and wished me well.

August 21, 2003

I went down to the retirement center yesterday and signed the papers to retire from the State of Ohio after 32+ years of civil service, including 11 months working for the Post Office. November will be the final month for me and then I am retired. I was shaking a bit yesterday, wondering if I was doing the right thing, wondering if I'll have enough money, and wondering if I'll get bored or find some things to keep me occupied.

August 23, 2003

I told the assistant deputy executive director this afternoon that I was retiring in November, and he seemed genuinely sad—surprised me. Then I told the director of the Bureau of Vocational Rehabilitation and she began to cry and got up to hug me, crying a bit on my shoulders. She told me that she remembers when she was an intern at the agency and we met. She said that she will genuinely miss me and that I was a bedrock for her when she saw me walk the halls. Even on her worst days, if she saw me, she felt okay. Sounds a bit melodramatic, but who am I to judge her feelings. Blew me away!

August 28, 2003

I am also feeling a bit sad and frightened. I am seemingly leaving my career in government vocational rehabilitation after 32.5 years. That is a long time, and yet, where did the time all go? Frightened, not only about the money issue but, maybe more importantly, what will I do with myself? Will I feel compelled to counsel or teach? I would rather teach than do private counseling, and even that is a maybe.

September 19, 2003

A good number of people at the Ohio Rehabilitation Association Conference in Dayton came up to wish me well in my retirement and to tell me that they will really miss me. I'll bet that at least seven or eight rehabilitation supervisors from around the state told me that the field counseling and supervisory staff will miss my input and impact on their work. One of the supervisors said that the field trusted me and felt that I had their best interests at heart. I had "been there in the trenches" and never forgot my roots.

October 31, 2003

Over the years, I worked with thousands of consumers and tried to help them fulfill their dreams. Having suffered a traumatic head injury and several bouts of severe depression myself, I understood fear and anxiety and tried to empathize with their life situations. Many of these men and women had a definite impact on my own life, especially on my spirituality. They made the Body of Christ[6] real for me. I thank them and ask their forgiveness for the times I may have failed them.

I want to thank God for his grace in my life. I thank him for my intelligence, my counseling and listening skills, my compassion, my perseverance, and for leading me into my career in vocational rehabilitation. What better career could one have than to help persons with disabilities become more independent and successfully employed? I don't know of one.

Farewell retirement speech, November 20, 2003

This morning, I went to the Center of Vocational Alternatives to speak to their Job Readiness class. The instructor wanted me to talk about my own experience with major depression and how I continued to be successful on the job. I talked for about 45 minutes and then opened it up for questions. It went well.

Afterwards, the instructor took me to her office, where she told me that it was very "right-on" and pertinent. She thanked me for making it "real" for her consumers. She asked if I would come back and talk to her new class next month, and I said, "Of course, I love doing this!"

April 12, 2006

I told the chairperson of the Sociology Department at the University that I was reading some books in preparation of maybe offering a course, An Overview of the Sociology of Disability. She liked the idea, and we talked a bit about how to structure it. I would like to offer it next year.

August 28, 2008

I'm going to forward a first draft of a syllabus on the Sociology of Disability course to the chairperson of the Sociology Department and see what she thinks. I am in such an approach-avoidance place inside. I think of teaching the course and maybe I could do a good job, and then I react inside emotionally in fear of the same. Here I am—a 60-year-old man who worked in the field for over 30 years, and I'm afraid I will do a poor job and be shown as a fraud. Oh, the old demons rise again!

January 30, 2009

Have been working more on my course on the Sociology of Disability and hope it goes okay. I wish I felt more confident in my abilities but accept that my feelings of inadequacy are there and I have to move on in spite of them. The course is taking more shape, although [it] needs some tweaking.

July 19, 2009

While my natural inclination would be not to put down what I am going to say, and while my natural inclination would be to dismiss or minimize what I am going to say, I think it is important to acknowledge it and to say it without embellishing or dismissing what I feel: This morning, I actually enjoyed teaching my class!

September 10, 2009

I was in training today to get six more CEUs[7] to keep my licenses and certifications up to date. One of the things I heard was a story by the instructor, who is a therapist. He once saw a man who had had a traumatic brain injury and as a result, the man had difficulty with any change. When he was forced to make a change on something, the therapist "held his hand" and got him through it. After a few weeks in the transition, the man was comfortable and got on with life. Boy, this sounds like me. I hate change and am a mess during the transition. My attorney says, "Joe, you just torture yourself." I never thought that it might be connected to my own traumatic brain injury in 1966.

September 2, 2010

I often feel that I've wasted the skills God gave me. I have counseling skills that I don't use professionally. During my career, I often did not try new things because I let my fears rule me, thinking that I had to have the right answer. But if I let myself sit with this confusion, then I see something else. I do use my counseling skills, albeit differently. I don't sit in an office and listen to people every hour tell me of their fears and issues, but I do listen to others when they talk to me, ask my counsel, ask my insights, and I give them my time. I give them a safe space to voice their concerns so that they can go "deeper" into their own being, listening to their own Shadow, their own spirit [and Spirit]. My aging neighbor comes to mind. And my career in vocational rehabilitation was done well. I did help probably thousands over 24 years as a vocational rehabilitation counselor.

December 27, 2006

1. The Catholic concept of reparation understands sin as a broken relationship with God that can always be healed. Humbly embracing one's human frailty, rather than denying it or projecting it onto another person, is one way to restore this relationship with God and God's people.

2. Cognitive therapy teaches that a person's thoughts result in feelings and then actions. If individuals can change their thinking, then they can change their feelings and actions.

3. The Morning Offering is a Catholic devotional practice that expresses the conscious desire to shape every thought, word, deed, and experience into a continuous act of loving worship.

4. "Offer it up" is a traditional Catholic expression encouraging the union of one's sufferings with the Cross of Jesus Christ in the conviction that this union is life-giving.

5. While the Catholic Church formally recognizes certain individuals as models of holiness by canonizing them as saints, it also believes that everyone is called to holiness (wholeness). It is in this sense that the members of the Church are referred to as the "communion of saints."

6. Although the Body of Christ technically refers to the union of Jesus Christ with all his followers in a community not bound by geography, I include people of other faiths and people of no faith. My clients, therefore, belong to the Body of Christ.

7. Continuing Educational Units are required to maintain a professional license or certification.

4

AFRAID OF INTIMACY

I'm saying I'm frustrated because I go to the baths and don't have a lover. And yet when the concept of an intimate relationship even appears on the horizon of my insides, I run away. I am truly afraid of intimacy in that sense.
April 29, 1977

I had homosexual thoughts and feelings as far back as I could remember. Even before I entered grade school, I can recall dreaming of Roy Rogers at night when I went to sleep. I purposely thought of him as I laid my head on my pillow. In my mind, Roy wore an open shirt and tight jeans and was lying on the ground face-up. I would lie on top of him, imagining that my genitals were near his. Feeling warm and secure, I soon went to sleep.

Unpublished Autobiography

[*Letter to my clinical psychologist on what was happening:*]
Dear Doctor,

I'm sitting at my desk wishing I could cry. I have been so hyper this morning that I thought I would pop. I want to die and I know (?) that this way I will commit suicide in time. Yesterday's session was good although depressing. It was good because I remember really feeling my "smallness" and "inadequacy." When I left I thought about that and also other things we talked about. You said that I wanted someone to hug me and that was why I was so affected by that movie where the boy was hugged. You're right!—I want to be hugged and caressed and protected. When I go to Cleveland (the baths) I am paid attention to and hugged and caressed. (As I write this I cry.)

Also my desire to be unhappy. I never really faced it but it is more coming to my consciousness. The warm secure feeling I get when I'm unhappy is secure and it is something. My mother—her philosophy somehow comes in there with mortification and sacrifice. So do Christianity and the cross but somehow that doesn't seem right.

God! I can't stand this. Everything is so screwed up and I'm so backward made. I wish I had never been born.

Joe

P.S. It's depressing to "see" a person with so many good things about him—good human feelings—be fucked up to such a degree.

September 21, 1973

[*From a letter to Fr. John McNeill, S.J., after reading his article, "The Homo-sexual and the Church," in the October 5, 1973, issue of the* National Catholic Reporter:]

Dear Fr. John McNeill,

I was raised a Catholic and my parents are good Catholics. My training in grade school and high school was considered traditional Catholic training and it was warped in sexual areas. I was taught that to play with my body was a mortal sin. I learned this in first grade. Being a sensitive person who wanted to "be good" I bought it. Even my curiosity play with the neighbors at that young age was tainted with this belief. I would feel extremely guilty and made sure that all my "partners" went to confession if they were Catholic.

During this time there were few boys around me with whom to play. I played mostly with the girl next door—house—and I dressed up accordingly. The boys in the Cub Scout Troop that I joined played sports but I felt quite awkward and did not really enjoy it. My forte then became school and studying. I did well and I still am quite a good student.

When I was young, I wanted to be a priest. That was my ideal. I kept the ideal until I was in high school. I applied for admission to an Order seminary[1] during my senior year in high school but was turned down because "you are too nervous and too sensitive." That decision was rather traumatic for me. Within six weeks of that rejection I masturbated for the first time to orgasm and could not believe my bodily reaction. Of course I felt guilty and the priest helped me to continue to foster that belief.

While at a Catholic college in the city, I went to see a guidance counselor and a priest about my masturbation and related topics. I was instructed by the counselor to come to him and tell him that if I masturbated I was being selfish and turning inward. At times during that year I brought up my feelings of homosexuality but they were dismissed as normal. I knew inside that they were not according to what others were feeling. The second year I met a priest who became my spiritual director full time. He helped me a lot and showed me that I was lovable and worthy in myself. He, too, however, kept trying to get me to see that I was worth more than masturbation, a type of activity that was demeaning to me. I did try, but the longest time I did stop was seven weeks.

The summer of my sophomore year in college I worked at a summer camp for underprivileged kids. It was too much for me emotionally. I was not sports-minded and to help these kids in this area only increased my feeling of inadequacy. Shortly after that I was in an adult theater and had my first homosexual contact. I remember going immediately to confession and having the priest mention nothing about the contact. He was only concerned with the masturbation. "I do not mean to scare you, son, but if you do not stop, you will lose your mind and go crazy." In my emotional turmoil, that did not help.

I arranged to seek professional help and after consulting various people that I trusted, I chose a clinical psychologist in the city with a very good reputation and who is an associate professor of psychiatry at The Ohio State University.

November 24, 1973

I went into weekly reparative, or conversion, therapy[2] from the fall of 1968 until the summer of 1974, and I paid for it myself with the money I made at a little part-time job I had while I attended college. The therapist used techniques from different psychotherapeutic theories. I was trained to believe that what I was really feeling wasn't homosexual per se but feelings of inadequacy as a man. Every time I had a [homosexual] fantasy or thought, I was taught to say I was just feeling inadequate. I participated in an aversion-therapy technique so that I could learn to associate any homosexual fantasy with something negative and uncomfortable. I was given medicine to stop all of my physical ejaculations and trained to make love to a plastic adult female doll. I was instructed to date women with a hierarchy of sexual and nonsexual behaviors. I had sexual relations with some women but never found it emotionally satisfying.

From the talk "The Grace of God in the Life on One Gay Catholic Man," given at the Call To Action of Michigan Conference, October 8–9, 1999

I had thought rather naïvely as I began therapy in 1968 that I would be heterosexual in a year. If the only criterion had been willpower, I would have been.

Unpublished Autobiography

[*Letter to Fr. John McNeill continues:*]
Finally, after about five years, my clinical psychologist told me that if I had another contact maybe I really wanted to try to live that way and maybe we should look at that. I stopped any homosexual activity from that day and continued for one year and a half. During that year I would try to re-orient myself. If I was masturbating, right before orgasm I would look at female stimuli and try to change my fantasies. Sometimes it worked; often it did not.

I did see a few prostitutes and tried working things out there. Once, I remember I was with a prostitute and I did enjoy the feelings. I was not able to "come" with her probably because I had masturbated the night before. But after forty-five minutes with her, I switched the fantasy to a man and got my insides started and then switched back to her. I had a beautiful orgasm and have never felt so emotionally and physically satisfied. Several people, who did not know where I had been, remarked how calm I looked. That incident gave the doctor and myself much hope for change.

However I kept trying and I was changing, according to the doctor. I was moving in the direction of heterosexuality. I guess I got discouraged and tired, though. Every time I got a homosexual feeling I would try my best to get rid of it. The tension level would increase and I would masturbate. Sometime last August something happened. I had been trying, and, to me, something wasn't working anymore. Even the day the doctor told me that I was moving in the direction of heterosexuality it just didn't matter. I told him I wanted to see if I would react the same way as I had before if I had a homosexual contact. He said that if I felt I wanted to, OK. So I did. It was as if I opened Pandora's box. I could not bury all those feelings again. I had more than one contact.

Within a matter of weeks I heard about the Club Baths[3] in Cleveland and went there about three times. Of course, free and easy sex and the idea of going where others felt just like me was exciting. So I went—but was depressed the next day, even to the point where I would think about suicide. I would make promises not to go out again, but Pandora's box was opened and I could not keep those promises to myself. Finally, I decided that I had to let the feelings go where they wanted for a while. I could not keep all that inside anymore. The doctor had mentioned to me long before this that maybe I should let myself live homosexually for a while and see if I really felt fulfilled by it. I never let myself have that possibility, even in my mind. However, during this time I decided that maybe I should look at it. However, my Catholic religion, and ethics and natural law[4] kept stirring me up inside.

This period of homosexual feelings and trying to work and reconcile them to my church was very difficult. It was really by accident that I picked up your article at the Newman Center[5] and it gave me such hope and it freed me to let myself experience myself; it gave me the religious "okay" to experience myself in this area. I guess from that point, the commitments not to go out lost their meaning.

I have to let go and see what I am inside. I went back to see that man I had sex with the first night I went out last August. We talked and we loved. He has been living with someone for fourteen years but has sex with others too. He admits to being a hedonist although he respects my beliefs. For the past several weeks I have had sex with him but not just sex. I try to express myself—I have shared with him me—my poetry, my feelings, my beliefs, and attitudes. I was really surprised the first time I shared with him my writings—he cried, really cried, he was so touched by them. Anyway, since then, if I have a homosexual feeling it is okay and I don't manipulate my mind trying to get rid of it. My masturbation has decreased, I suppose, for two reasons. If I know that I will be seeing him then my sexual needs will be taken care of. Also, however, my anxiety level had decreased and the need to masturbate to relieve it is decreased.

Since I have stopped fighting my homosexual urges and even given expression to them, I find that it would be easier, I think, to be moral and to integrate them into my being. For me, these feelings seem natural.

November 24, 1973

I think that Scripture could be talking to me when it says that not everyone who says, "Lord, Lord," will get to heaven but only those that do the will of the Father. I want to get to heaven. I want my God, but I want me, too, the real me, and if that self is sinner, then God will have to accept me, the sinner. I just hope he puts me in his Christ and misses the sin.

November 28, 1973

Somehow, I don't accept the fact that I am sexually attractive to some females. To accept that would challenge some of my self-image and my thought patterns and actions. I do dress nicely and fashionably. I can act flirty and I guess even unconsciously try to turn girls on or make them like me. However, I block letting myself fully accept this as being anything more than a game. I block letting myself accept the response. My clothes, my hair, my nice looks, my flirtations are all external. When I start to look inside, I block it and resist it. Even my homosexual feelings are filler; they are avoidance of this other deeper part.

March 3, 1974

I sit at my desk and listen to very romantic music on the radio. Although my sexual life is oriented towards males, it seems much of my feeling romantic side is female. I sit with a woman in my lap, holding her warm body. It feels good even though I get no erection or sexually stimulated. Too bad I can't get them both one way or the other comfortably.

May 12, 1974

I met a priest in Dayton, Ohio, at the workshop "The Gay Christian: Developing a Ministry to Homosexuals." I really fell for him. As soon as I saw him, I wanted to see more of him—inside. Later, the relationship became physical, which only added to the beauty of it. I certainly did not intend to feel all this. I guess I just opened myself a little and out I came. It was beautiful and yet very painful. This man was so free, and I want to be that free. He was a good man and very moral. He was much more decent than I, and to see him made me feel as if my Christianity is a mockery. I will probably never see him again, as he lives far from here.

June 17, 1974

I want to like myself, to affirm myself, and to be able to say and really believe that I am okay. I want to be able to affirm my gayness even if I didn't ever act on it again. I've got to affirm myself and get on with the business of living my life. I am a good person with a lot of good characteristics, and I won't really affirm them for all this other "game" I do with the other parts of me.

July 5, 1974

Over the evening, I had a beer and five Singapore Slings, plus dinner. A colleague from work kept after me to unload what was bothering me. He heard me tell of my frustration at work but knew it was something else. I became more defensive, and yet the drinks were working on me. I remember saying that if I told people, they would ostracize me. He told me that I was hoping they knew but didn't want to say what it was. I said yes, that this was true—I wanted to scream it out but couldn't. He kept after me to go ahead. He also said if this was damaging to me, he would stop. Well, I knew I wasn't going to tell him, so I said no. Toward the end of the evening, he and another colleague met two waitresses they know and joined them. While the two girls were talking, my friend kept staring at me and kept urging me to talk. I asked him if he knew, and he said yes. Then a little later, he asked, "Are you a fag?" and I just looked at him and said no. But my nerves were shot, and this morning, I was standing at the mirror and my legs just shook. I want to tell people, but I'm afraid of it. At the same time, I know that to free myself, I must be true to who I am for myself and others.

March 5, 1975

I got the Dignity6 newsletter tonight and withdrew from it. I don't want to hear about how they want to counter anti- and inhuman behavior of gays such as going to bed with people you don't even know. [The newsletter] talked about how it is more difficult to open oneself emotionally and psychologically to another than it is just to go to bed. However, that is where I'm at now. I'm afraid of relationship—I don't want to be limited or held down.

March 11, 1975

Suicide thoughts have been running in my mind for a good while lately. I scare myself with them because I think I could do that easily. My feelings change so. And then I say, "See, you are really sick!"

March 19, 1975

Well, I went to the baths in Toledo. It took me three hours to drive there. When I was there, I didn't want to cum too soon but finally went ahead in the dry steam room. A little later, I went to bed because I was tired. Then I got up refreshed and went to bed with someone else. I played around a little, but I guess I didn't really want sex, either. I had planned to spend the whole night but left at ten o'clock for the trip home. I stopped at rest areas, looking for something, and it was all compulsive. The fact that it is compulsive bothers me and tells me, "Joe, you're sick!" I was refreshed, though, when I left the baths. I felt good and relaxed. Of course, driving three hours back made me tired. I felt guilty, however, about going. First, it was compulsive. Second, I had intended going to the Good Friday services and could have done without sex. But I went to the baths and wasted my money and my time. However, to show some inconsistency maybe, I did fast yesterday somewhat.

March 29, 1975

You know, I'm a touching person, really. Been thinking of the man I met and had sex with but that I keep pushing away even though I know he is a nice guy. Maybe I'll always resist relationships and stay alone. Maybe I'll be a monk. Or, just to make myself say it, maybe I'll meet someone, fall in love, and work with him in making our lives praise the Father and grow in love of each other. There! This is Easter, and Easter is a feast of hope. Jesus lives, and he lives in us. He has conquered eternal death, and we can live in love with each other and with God forever.

March 30, 1975

For the past three days, I've been on a promiscuous run for sex. Tonight, I saw the next-door neighbor come out of the house with his wife. They looked at the lilac bush and kissed. I couldn't seem to see enough of them. Everything ached inside, and I wanted the closeness and yet, I reject it. It's impossible, and I want to strike at it. I want a relationship, but the man I'm interested in is not interested in me. Suicide has been on my mind for weeks, and the fantasy of taking a gun to my throat lingers. I guess I really and truly believe I'll end up doing that someday. A part of me hates my gayness, hates my promiscuity, hates everything.

May 6, 1975

I went with a group to a gay bar in Dayton and danced. I have difficulty meeting new people and don't really go up to others in the bar if I don't know them. I never know what to say and how to do small talk, so going with the group makes things much more enjoyable. While there, I met a guy and was attracted to him right off and he liked to dance. We danced slowly, two or three times, and he fit right into my arms. God, I love to dance that way. I remember having difficulty in my mind, however, while all this was going on because of the thought of becoming a monk. I kept thinking what would happen if I really met someone that I liked. Something inside me said I would want to go with him, and something else said inside that it would not be enough. I would have to try the other just to make sure.

July 21, 1975

51

My God,
I feel lonely today and have for several weeks.
My insides cry out for relief from this alienation.
My spirit begs for someone to touch my insides, to warm them, to fill them up.
Today, when I was at Mass,⁷ I looked up to the cross
and for a few brief moments
saw myself bound to it. I felt my insides pinned to the very center.
I felt like I was being crucified, and maybe I was and maybe I am, for I am
involved in your paschal mystery.
The music I listen to on my stereo pulls me in many different directions.
The pictures I look at do the same. I want someone to love, to touch,
to give my life to.
Father, do you hear me? I know that you hear me, but will you answer me—
soon?

October 26, 1975

Father,
help me to open up my arms to you, to life, to myself.
Help me, please, to meet a man to whom and for whom I may live my life,
a man who also loves me and will share his life with mine.
Help me, please, to grow and to reflect your beauty in this world of suffering,
loss, and turmoil.

May 6, 1976

Father,
my insides hurt. I have so much to give,
and yet I don't seem to be able to utilize it right now.
My insides desire to meet another and to melt with him.
They desire peace and rest, Father.
Grant me your soothing balm. Dear God, don't lose me, please.
Your son, Joe.

May 16, 1976

Went to bed with a man I've been pursuing for a while. We just listened to the classical music on the stereo. Because he may have been reexposed to syphilis, we were extra careful. However, the big thing is that we were both so relaxed and I was so comfortable lying in his arms, my head slightly on his chest, my hands softly traveling his chest and stomach. He was affectionate and tender with me. He kissed me on my forehead and pulled me close to him.

How good the body is. How sacred it is, and holy. I don't think the Church really appreciates the incarnation of Christ. God's action showed us that matter is good, our bodies are good, and sex is a vehicle for intimacy and touching.

May 23, 1976

I have a strange feeling that I will end up like one of my aunts—alone and miserable. Self-fulfilling prophecy? I don't know, but I do recognize a real self-hatred streak in me. It's not that I necessarily hate myself. It's just that I'm tired, tired of all the trying, the hassles, the struggles, the pain. I'm just tired.

May 31, 1976

I want to integrate myself, Lord.
I want to integrate my sexuality and become more whole, more human,
and more contemplative.
I am well aware of my inclination toward the easy, towards promiscuous sex
as an avoidance of confronting self, of confronting my aloneness
and oftentimes loneliness,
and avoidance of my void. Help me to deal with them
and know that I am not alone.
I can face them; I can face me because you are with me and have made me strong.

June 20, 1976

I feel guilty or unsatisfied this morning after two hours last night at the baths. I have felt this too often lately, and I don't like the feeling. I am not sure, however, what I would do, not having sex with another person. I don't know what would happen to my insides if I didn't go to the baths. Probably nothing as awful as I envision.

I think that I can now make a decision not to go to the baths but to let my feelings of unrest, of frustration, of fear be. At least, I now want to try. Going to the baths is an avoidance of that horrible aloneness and sense that I'm not going to make it. However, I do make it and then have to contend with this feeling of short-circuitness and this feeling that I am still unfulfilled, that my sexual activities are not a deep expression of me.

June 22, 1976

I am afraid for myself. What is to happen to me as I grow older? A gay magazine, the *Advocate*, had an article last issue about aging, and it said that individuals should build up a number of friendship relationships. I guess, in a way, I don't do that. I am a loner, and I know it. I also tend to short-circuit the time it takes to build relationships. Either I am so emotionally touched that I come on too strong, or I tend towards promiscuous and impersonal sex—no names, please.

July 3, 1976

Had a good session with my psychologist. Went to work and then to Mass. After Mass, I got in the car to come home, but the thought of having sex was titillating. So, had sex. Was aware that the feeling for sex sometimes comes after a feeling of a desire to union—such as a desire for union with my God. Maybe the feeling for union comes in and I relieve it or express it through sex with another human being. I'll try to watch and observe more carefully in the future.

July 6, 1976

I desire union—union with God and union with my fellow man. I do not handle well this gnawing for union, this drive towards wholeness. I seek that which will not satisfy, and yet, in all my searchings for satisfaction, for unity, I am yearning for my God where I will be satisfied, I will be full.

July 14, 1976

I was awed and humbled last night by my ability to really help a neighbor who needed to talk. I guess I don't believe it just happened. I believe it was supposed to happen and the Spirit was working in me helping my neighbor. That happened earlier this week, for I was a good counselor for a client at work. I thought of just getting in touch with my feelings after my neighbor left last night, but I couldn't. I drove to the baths but stopped on the way so I could help a stranded motorist. Everything was saying, "Don't go to the baths. Stay with your feelings." But I didn't listen, and I don't know why. I kept thinking that my going to the baths last night was a way of neutralizing the feeling that I am a good man and God does work in me. I shirk my responsibility that way.

Another thing I notice is that the desire for sex always comes after a real emotional experience of my humanity like what happened last night with my neighbor. It crosses my mind that if I stayed with the feeling after those experiences, I might even have a further mystical or religious experience. I don't know about that—all I know is I get rid of the feeling and never get satisfied by the sex. Instead, I go into a downer emotionally.

I must learn to stay and accept that powerful religious experience and let it be, let me be held by it and floated along. There really is a job I am supposed to do, and I think it has to do with people as helper. I am doing it now, but I feel called to a deeper experience of my humanity and by a more mystical experience of my participation in the Cosmic Christ. I lay before the Father for his healing my infidelity to the call to listen to my insides and get closer to them. The closer I get to my insides, the more real, I think, will be my experience of God.

August 7, 1976

I am sitting in my living room, stereo on, telephone buried under blankets so I will not hear it. I am aware of my void, of my aloneness, of my loneliness, of so many decisions, so many unfufillments (sigh). For right now, I will accept it. Love yourself, Joe; be kind to yourself; be at peace.

November 9, 1976

I am more aware of my aloneness at this time of the year, and yet, I accept it right now. I want to own myself, all of me, the together parts, the loose ends, the satisfied facets, my depressed facets.

December 25, 1976

I have been avoiding touching my insides for a good while lately. I'm running, and I just don't want to look yet. Part is the fact that I know relationships scare me. I talk much of loneliness and my desire to have another person. At the same time, I am realizing I enjoy being alone, too. I enjoy being independent, on my own schedule, with my own interests. I don't feel tied this way, and should I decide to leave or whatever, I can with only myself to worry about. I think this fear of relationship goes deeper. It even enters just the sphere of friendship; it enters the realm of intimacy. I'm afraid.

February 2, 1977

At the baths, I have been intimate in the physical and emotional sense with others, but there is no commitment past the time I am with them. Even sometimes there, too, I must catch myself. If I'm with one person and someone else who attracts me more, walks by, I can feel my insides wanting to get up and leave. That happened a week ago, but I told myself to stay in the present, to see about the person I was with. Interestingly, he was quite nice and also good in bed. I think I miss out on a good number of things that way: I don't stay in the present, for one, but live often in the future. And two, I'm unrealistic, looking for "Mr. Wonderful" to come along and fulfill my needs.

April 29, 1977

Sex is a tension-releaser for me, but having sex with a person is more fulfilling than alone. To masturbate releases the tension physically, but to have sex with a person involves more of me. My skin-hunger is satisfied as I touch and hug another and allow myself to be touched and held and made love to. It seems almost as if my insides, my inner organs, become satisfied, too. Of course, I still feel guilty about the baths, not morally, maybe, as much as psychologically. I'm afraid that going to the baths is not healthy because there is no relationship, because I satisfy my needs by using sex and I do it whenever I want to. I guess I may see this as setting up a pattern of instant gratification, and that scares me.

May 1, 1977

I don't usually question my gayness anymore. That is a given, but I do wonder about all my promiscuity. Because of the hell I went through years ago with dos and don'ts given by priests and others, I have difficulty accepting new ones today. Also, with my psych background, I am also more careful. I can and do see sin in my feelings with people and myself, in the concrete areas of interaction, of justice and charity. But I don't tend to see sin (and I guess I don't want to) in many sexual expressions. Somehow, though, I think it would be far better and healthier, physically and psychologically, to have a faithful partner. I'm traditional enough to find value there.

May 28, 1977

I am aware that I somehow do not know how to be intimate. By my attitudes and behaviors, mostly but not all unconscious, I place barriers up against intimacy.

March 14, 1978

When talking with my psychologist yesterday, I mentioned that meeting one of the spa instructors, to whom I'm attracted not just physically, but emotionally, has shown me that I am still alive and that I guess I still have some hope that I may meet someone someday to love and who loves me. Underneath all my cynicism and defense, I want to be in union with another human being.

March 22, 1978

I was afraid to go to New York. I always am nervous before any change in my normal routine. But I got on the plane and landed at LaGuardia around noon. I took a bus to the East Terminal and a cab to the "Y." Shortly after getting settled there, I knew that I wanted sex. It almost seems like I need to get that out of the way first so that I can concentrate on other things. Maybe it was also because NYC has so much of it. Anyway, I went down to the Village and just began to walk around. The gay bars were everywhere, and people seemed so free and easy about who they are. In a relatively short time, I found the Christopher Street Bookstore (the one that I have seen so many advertisements for) and went in. It is a very good porno bookstore with a backroom for those who are interested and can pay an extra dollar. I paid the dollar, went in, and had sex.

I then kept walking, feeling much more relaxed. I came to a park, and there were so many of the "brothers" that I didn't quite know how to take it all in. Everyone seemed so free, and they were so easy to talk to. I began to talk to this blond man about how great his city was. He agreed. He then pointed out the piers, which I had heard so much about. They are really dangerous at night, but this was early afternoon. So I went over to see them and found them somewhat busy. I had sex there, too. The interesting thing about that was that I had a great conversation and felt intimacy with this man, even in the midst of easy sex.

Gay persons—some gay persons—seem to have a more relaxed attitude toward sexuality and sexual relationships. I am not sure how I feel about that, but I know that I have that attitude too. I am not hurting anyone and see no reason at this point not to let myself experience different people. I cannot look to the Church for guidance on the matter since her head is so erophobic and back in the Dark Ages.

Later, I went back to the "Y" to clean up and to rest. I was tired since I had not slept very well for the previous two or three nights. I was to meet a friend about seven o'clock, and I did. He looked great, and I really enjoyed seeing him. We went back to the Village and just relaxed. I couldn't get over men walking with other men, hugging each other and kissing each other on the streets. Lesbians, too. It was so natural.

On Thursday, I continued to walk. I went by New York University and stopped in their chapel. It is quite pretty. I walked all over and saw shop after shop. I bought a ring with the Lambda symbol (λ)[8] on it. I also bought a leather wristband. I went to several bookstores, including Oscar Wilde. I spent over $60 for books on homosexuality.

Friday night, my friend and I went to the Dignity/Integrity Dance in the Village. It was so good to be with my brothers and sisters in a very human manner and then to have that dance in the midst of Greenwich Village, the gay haven of NYC. My mind was being blown away, and I had a hard time even fathoming it all. At one point, I was out in the courtyard watching it all and without pre-thought, I raised my eyes and forearms to the sky and, in prayer, said, "Thank God, I am gay."

On Saturday, I walked a bit before breakfast and then went to the Club Baths. It was beautiful, and I met a very nice man. I did not have sex with him but had coffee for about an hour. He was a disc jockey from North Carolina, and we had a very interesting talk. He had a lover back home and wanted to tell his parents who he was. I told him some of my story, and that may have helped. I reaffirmed in my own head how truly grateful I am for coming out at work, at home, and at my church. It is good to be who you are, regardless of how others see it. I will not live a double life for anybody!

That afternoon, I went with Dignity to St. Patrick's Cathedral to protest the stance of the Roman Catholic Church in the Diocese of New York against the gay rights ordinance coming up for a vote. Later, I met my friend and we walked some more. It was so good for me to see my brothers holding hands and walking together in such an open and human fashion. It was also great to see such beautiful bodies. The guys work out a lot in New York, and it shows.

Sunday morning, I was in the Village bright and early for the Gay Pride March. Soon, my friend and others met up with me. The streets were crowding up, and the excitement in the air was wonderful. The police stood by to keep things in an orderly fashion, but they were really great. No funny remarks, no funny looks.

Then to Central Park for the big rally. We left shortly thereafter and got back to the Village for the Christopher Street Festival. I just couldn't believe it. Lovers, male and male, female and female, were walking everywhere together. It was a most natural sight for me, and I just kept contrasting it to the scene back in Columbus, Ohio. Across from me sat two really masculine men who were the "commercial" types. They were extremely good-looking, and they were being quite affectionate with each other. I finally got up, went over, and told them how beautiful they were in the sharing of affection. They beamed and thanked me.

I took a walk by myself to the piers. I had sex while I was there. Later, I went back to the street festival, where there was a crowd listening to music. Some conga drum players were playing the drums with other rhythmic instruments going along. Pretty soon, several of us were just letting go and dancing in the place. It was so freeing and liberating and human. There were just no inhibitions like there are in Columbus. It was wonderful.

I went back to the "Y" to take a shower and get cleaned up. Then I came back to the festival and saw some people I had met in the march. I stayed with them for a while. I met a man there who was very sensitive, and I spent most of the rest of the evening with him. He knew Fr. John McNeill, who had really helped him to accept his homosexuality and to integrate it. He had been in therapy with Fr. McNeill and is now a psychotherapist. We had a common cord right off.

He told me that he didn't go to Communion anymore but that when he went to bed at night, he prayed to God, "I really want to love you." He was so simple, so sincere, that he moved me practically to tears. We went to the park and just held each other. People walked by, but everyone else was gay and nobody thought a thing of it. It was so natural to me, and I again affirmed myself. I left him later on and went back to the "Y." He did not have a place to go so that we could lie together, and I didn't either. Having sex with him would have been far more intimate than the sex that I had been having.

That evening, I went to the Mineshaft Bar. It was a bar and sex palace for gay people into some of the extremes of the gay world. Almost everything went on there. It shocked me and scared me. I don't think I want to go back.

On Monday, I went to Ellis Island to see where my relatives came over to this country. Afterwards, I walked around the Wall Street area for a while. On Tuesday, I took a tour of Rockefeller Plaza and was even on the elevator of the Center with Nelson Rockefeller. I then met with Dr. Ralph Blair of the Homosexual Counseling Center for about an hour and a half to discuss my life and schooling. Wednesday, I flew back to Columbus.

I am still high from the trip. I am glad that I am gay, and I thank God for the gift of my homosexuality. It is very good to be who I am, a gay male.

Thank you, Father.

July 2, 1978

I sit here in the chapel at Gethsemani Abbey. I look at the monks file into choir. It really is impressive on one level. I watch young men who have been here for years, and I wonder how they have done it; I wonder what they have done to their sexuality and its expression. I wonder where they are in their prayer life.

Years ago I would come and pine away because I wanted to be here. I was not at peace with myself. Now I come, still wondering the same questions but without the pining. This is not my vocation, even if there is attraction on one level. My call is to be in the world, helping my brothers and sisters. Exactly how this is to be done, I am not sure.

I am aware that I have broken through my barrier of self-hatred because of my gayness. When I first came to this monastery years ago, I hated myself as a gay man. Today I sit here and thank God for his gift to me, his gift of gayness. I thank him for his gift of my unique personality, my counseling skills, my attitudes and outlooks. I am [in] awe that I was able to break through the barrier.

July 15, 1978

I didn't sleep too well last night. When I awoke, I was cold; my dreams had been at the Mineshaft in NYC. I got up and went to Matins at 3:15 a.m. in the Abbey church. I am tired and yet I am awake. I love the silence of the early morning. It is a deep silence.

I am also aware of the places in NYC, which are open all night long, places that I visited—the baths, bars, and bookstores. I do not judge it; it is also a part of who I am. It is another part of my world through which the Spirit flows.

July 16, 1978

Adam is out tonight with a friend. Before he left, he received a phone call from his wife. He upset himself with it and went through the conversation with me. He also had mixed feelings about going out with someone while staying in my home with me. While lying in the bed going over all this, he told me that he felt more comfortable with me. That felt good because it is a nice feeling for me to know I am able to provide "space" physically and psychologically for him here. When he left, he kissed me, told me he liked me, told me I was a nice person. What do I feel?

I feel sad tonight. Adam has begun to move in; I am packing to pursue my doctoral studies at Ohio University in Athens. It is somewhat disconcerting to leave. I am aware that I like Adam and want to get to know him better. I am letting myself be intimate and I am not scaring myself. My feelings are not "in love," and I am not sure I "love" him yet. When I use that word, I will mean it. I am aware he is the first person that I really think I could form a deep relationship with. I find myself wanting to give him space to grow and be himself. Maybe that is love! I do care for him.

I am aware that living in Athens, Ohio, will greatly minimize the frequency of our communication. I am afraid the relationship will wither into nothing. I am afraid he will fall in love with someone and "leave." But I need to let him be and to grow as he does. He is too nice a person to try to possess and manipulate. Important point is the fact that I am being inti-

60

mate with another human being. I am capable of deep affection; I am capable of love.

Adam and I kept touching and pretty soon were involved sexually. We had sex and I loved it. My sexual acts with Adam are much more than just acts. They are an expression of my feelings as well as my body. I like Adam and would like to have a deep relationship with him. Maybe I already do.

I am aware that I have really grown in my relationship with him. I am aware that I am being intimate with someone on a very deep level, involving sex, and am not scaring myself. I am letting another person in and allowing myself to become vulnerable. I find it wonderfully exciting. I am aware that I have a great deal to offer; I have the capability of deep love and deep affection for another person.

Adam and I talked a while and finally went to bed. We snuggled up to each other, and then he said, "I've become more human since I've been sharing your bed." Wow, what a compliment! And I can also return the compliment, for I have been much more integrated and whole with Adam in my home and bed. I need intimacy and relationships.

Father, do you hear me?

Adam is easy to talk to. I can be myself with him—strong, weak, secure, insecure, restless, and contented. He is a good friend. I also must admit that I feel more insecure because I am moving, rooting up my stakes, giving up my job, going back to school. I find it all disconcerting, but I'll try to flow with it instead of clutching. Joe, let it be; flow with the process.

Have been quite emotionally intimate with Adam tonight. After we left home, we went to Rudely Elegant° to dance. It was wild, free, and earthy. I danced and released tension about school. Adam and I left and came home. He talked about his fear of me going, his fear of being alone without his wife. He spoke of my helping him to process, to keep in touch with his feelings. He asked me to help him keep in touch with me by writing and letting him know of how I feel.

When talking about how aware I am of my feelings, Adam said that it goes further than that. He said that I not only am in touch with them but I am also in process with them. I take the risk and share [my feelings] with others, which helps them get in touch with their own feelings. He told me that this was a gift.

I told Adam that I was afraid, scared of moving, not only because of school but also because I was leaving him. I told him that I have never been in a gay relationship in which I felt so human, so together, so integrated. I thanked him.

August 27, 1978

Adam helped me move down to Athens. He was so supportive. He stayed Sunday night and we had sex. Monday, I really became hyper and scared. Adam decided to stay the night and leave early this morning. At 5 he was up. I hated for him to go. We have lived together since June 17, and even though we have not been exclusive, we have developed an emotional bond with each other.

My future with Adam: will we grow apart or closer; will I lose out in love; will I be too busy to see him? I miss Adam as I sit here. I wonder how he is doing and what he is doing.

September 5, 1978

Saw Adam on Wednesday and noticed there was a difference in the relationship. I found out that Adam felt really tired after my last visit because he could not get through my mind-fucking. I realized, too, that his apartment is not mine at all anymore and the relationship is different. Adam is making friends, giving parties, and building his life up. I feel angry and insecure. I am jealous because when I lived there, I didn't do that. I didn't make that many friends, or, as Adam pointed out, maybe I did but didn't keep in touch. No, I didn't; I tended to end them. I was insecure because I felt (and still have the fear) that the relationship would end. I have created a dependency on Adam, which is not good at this point.

September 21, 1978

I have just gotten a letter from Adam. I literally shake as I type this note here. I feel a real sense of loss and distancing. Adam has asked that we not have any sex between us for the present now. He does not want to live with me in December. He will consider it only on the condition that I [use] his children's bed when they are not there and go somewhere else when they are there. I cannot accept his offer under those conditions for me.

He stated that he does not see this as ending or reducing the relationship but rather sees it as our present lifestyle. He mentioned that he still values me as a very dear and special friend, confidant, and stimulant.

I feel shaken, rootless, and insecure. What am I doing about it? I need to take what Adam is taking for himself: control of his life. I need to be a little selfish for me and to take care of my needs, too. I will try to adapt myself to Adam's schedule when I can. However, I must begin to do things for me and to be careful how it will affect my feelings and equilibrium.

November 3, 1978

Father, it hurts. Share my pain.

November 4, 1978

I think my relationship/friendship with Adam will continue if we are both honest, if we continue to communicate with each other, and if we both make time with and for each other. I am aware that he really is one of the deepest, maybe the deepest, friends that I have and I don't want to lose that friendship. I will do what I can to cultivate and strengthen it. I desire the relationship.

November 28, 1978

I wonder if I pressure Adam. I wonder what he feels. I don't want to pressure him, I really don't. My love for him is deep. I want his growth and development, and that means dating, loving, sex, and job. My "panic," my "clutching" comes not because I don't really want his growth. It's just my fear that we'll never be in "relationship," be together. I also fear I won't "grow" and develop as Adam does, being left behind.

December 10, 1978

I am aware that I pressured Adam, but only after he told me that I was. When I think about it, I must admit that I probably do and I push in this sense: Adam is quite vulnerable regarding his feelings about sex and intimacy. Therefore, if he tells me that something we are doing is "fine," that is his statement about where he is with it. I don't relate to "fine" because it is not really a "feeling" word to me. However, and this is important, that is my "thing." Adam is telling me that he is all right with his word, "fine"; he does not do the feeling thing as I do, and that is okay. It is a different style, regardless of why he has the style. When he tells me that I am pushing, what he is saying is that I am not accepting him where and how he is at that moment. I am looking for his communication in my terms, and I cannot do that. I want to let Adam be Adam, and I have to learn how to listen, really listen, to what he is saying in his terms, not mine.

December 23, 1978

God, I hurt, and I don't know what to do about it.
Please grant me your balm; soothe my breaking heart with your gentle hands,
Father.
I do want to believe in you. I do want to believe you, Father.

February 21, 1979

Dear Adam,

I got your letter of May 1. Needless to say, going from your April 25 letter with, "I don't have time for a relationship" and "my personal life is promiscuous" to your latest one with, "Peter and I have announced that we are lovers" was a jolt. With the history of our relationship, I would have liked to have been told differently. For one, I heard the news via the telephone from someone else before I heard it from you, and, two, I didn't expect to hear it in a "Dear John" letter under "other news." You could have done better, Adam.

Joe

May 6, 1979

I had been getting in touch with my Shadow. In Jungian psychology, the Shadow is the same sex as yourself, who comes out in dreams. He or she is the other side of you on the conscious level. For me, he is cruel, angry, and a part of me that I am not in tune with. I had noticed that in certain positions of sex, I got in touch with an anger that I had not been aware of previously. I was surprised, and yet others knew of this anger, or parts of it. A professor at Ohio University had pointed out to me how I swallowed people's comments to me which hurt but which I didn't do anything about. He said that he could see me laugh but my nonverbals showed hurt. I wasn't even aware of it.

When my confessor came to see me, we talked about it. He asked me if I had a name for my Shadow, and I said no. He asked me if I could see [my Shadow], and I said no. And then I saw him and named him. He was dressed in leather from top to bottom, with a leather vest covering his bare chest. He is cruel-looking and sadistic. My confessor told me that I need to dialogue with [my Shadow], but I didn't know how.

Interestingly, my Shadow, my Honcho Man, doesn't seem as scary as he did before I pictured him. At the same time, I am not completely comfortable with him either. I really don't know what to do with that. At one point, I tried to imagine the Mineshaft and things that I would do there. I hope to go to NYC in August and wonder whether I should go there with my Shadow, fully conscious, and see what happens.

June 15, 1980

Well, I went to NYC and I did act out. It almost seemed as if my Shadow took over at times. Not that I noticed so much anger, but I did notice I got in touch with a power, a power that I used to control, dominate, and manipulate people. This power came out in a sadistic way at times and also in the sexual scenes that I saw when I talked "dirty." I experienced real evil in myself in a way that I have not done before. I was powerful at times, but the power was "over" people, in control.

I think part of it is to put down other gays because there is still a part of my sexuality, of my personhood, that I want to put down. That is Shadow, and I need to integrate more. NYC is so pretty, so alive, so vibrant. It has such goodness to it and also such evil. It is almost symbolic of people, of me. I have goodness in me and also much evilness, such sin!

Late August 1980

Reading a book about angels and how they protect us if we ask them to, makes me think about the time I was in the Mineshaft in New York City in August of 1980. I think I had been there a while and may have had sex by this time, too, but I had a strong sense of evil there. It wasn't as if I felt that the people there were evil, but I had a strong sense that this wasn't right, that something was definitely off.

It was an interesting reaction inside, as I remember, because on many occasions before this I used to go there. I didn't see it as bad, necessarily. I felt that it was okay because I didn't have a partner and wasn't in a relationship. While there may have been some qualms, I know that my reactions were usually positive. That is why that one time when I felt such evil, it startled me and I think I left fairly soon after that reaction set in.

I believe that this sense could very well have been my angel taking care of me. AIDS was around then, and from the reports that I've read, it probably entered the USA around 1976. I could have been exposed to it on so many occasions, and somehow, I feel that my angel was warning me to get the hell out of there that night. This is just one of the stories in my life that makes me feel and believe that God has his hand on me and is not letting me go.

July 31, 1993

Dear Father-God,
help me to be free, to be a man, to be powerful in my gentleness.
I want to love me; I want to love you.
Your son, Joe.

September 2, 1980

Today I am at a workshop, part of which is stress management and bioenergetics. Well, part of the session was on anger release, and I let myself act out my anger by putting the energy in my arm and fist and getting into the words "God damn motherfucker, son of a bitch." I felt energized afterwards. So I will do it again. I think I have found a way that I can work on the anger a bit. Dialoguing with my Shadow is something that I am not clear on. I don't know how to do it, and yet maybe some of what I am doing is dialogue.

They had a dance at this conference, and once I started, I may have sat out 2 or 3 dances. I loved it and I felt powerful. Interesting, not put-down power—just self-assuredness. It's a different dancing than gay male slow dancing. It is freer, more flowing movement. How good I felt, and free!

September 9, 1980

Well, the past days have seen me get in touch with more anger at more levels. I am aware of something that strikes me. I did get in touch with more anger, and yet, I was praying at the same time. That seems significant to me for some reason—I really did ask Jesus to be with me, to come and enter my life—to become flesh of my flesh.

I can't rid myself of my gayness, and yet I know the pain of being different, of always being different. My being different also always meant "being less than" or "being inferior to." All my life, this has been my deepest experience, even when I received awards.

I went out to dinner with a friend and experienced his "difference," his torment in not being able to reconcile his desires for a "whole" body with the reality of his crippled one. I experienced again what it was like to want to be straight and not be able to. I also reexperienced, in a way, my surrender to that fact. Somehow, I felt more closure. Somehow, I feel I'm getting closer to integrating my Shadow, my Honcho Man. I think he has to do with my power, my strength. I almost got a glimpse of what that man would be like. Yes! A man, gay and whole, who loves others, his God, and himself. I want to be one with God, with others, and with myself. That desire is the same. That is wholeness; that is holiness. I want it!

September 17, 1980

Somehow, the baths aren't too good for me. It is so easy to let my Shadow out to begin to see people as objects for my pleasure and use. I don't like that about me. I want to really see them. I profess to be Christian, and yet that attitude inside is so unchristian. I went to Mass this morning and prayed for myself and others. I want to be good, to be whole, to be holy, but God, I am a sinner!

October 8, 1980

I got up early today to pray and to enjoy the silence of the night and early morning. Have found myself praying for something that surprises me. I have found myself praying for chastity. I'm not sure where this is coming from, and I must admit, it frightens me, but it has been involved in my prayer. I do want to be united with Jesus. I want to be saved; I want to be holy.

October 11, 1980

The baths used to be enjoyable for me, but I've noticed since NYC (and it was probably before that) that I am more aggressive there, less gentle, less interested in the other person as a person. I become selfish, superficial, "picky," and sometimes almost bitter. I use people for my needs more. I think that it used to be more a mutual thing, but not anymore.

October 16, 1980

I become more alive, more human, more open and whole when I am in a relationship with another person. I was a couple with Adam and felt it. I want a personal relationship with another man, and somehow, my growth is involved with it.

> *Please, Father, hear me, the voice of one who wants to be in you,*
> *flesh of your flesh, alive with your spirit flowing through me.*

December 16, 1980

I called a guy I met several weeks ago at the baths. He told me that he may be in a sex party that night and I'd be welcome. He told me to go to the Trade Winds (a leather bar) that night. I went all in leather and met him and his friends. I also met an acquaintance of mine there in leather. I tried on his leather jacket and I experienced my Honcho Man again. I experienced him, or at least a part of me that I could be or have been in another life. I felt powerful, attractive, and in control.

The group decided to hit the baths, and so did I. I'm aware that nothing happened that had anything to do with love, affection, or sex really. It

67

was a power game, and that's maybe what I liked so much. I suppose, too, that it felt good to be included in somebody's group. It felt good to be in touch with the power. It's strange, but when I put on that leather coat, it was almost like finding a lost part of me—it felt so natural, and yet I experienced some fear with it. It was almost as if I feel like I have to go leather— I have to let him out (will I lose my soul?). As I think here, I wonder if my evening was so wild because of that experience.

I'm still saying Lauds and Compline[10] and going to Mass a day or two during the week. After a night like the other night, however, I feel like such a hypocrite!

February 1, 1981

I haven't been able to get in touch with anger. But last night, I went to the baths. God, what anger! I turned it inward for one thing and engaged in "pushing the barriers" behavior. My anger came out in sex. I talked dirty, loud, and I just let it out. I'm aware as I think of it that I have a great deal of energy in my personality (I could be a dynamic person, but I don't use it) and I am very earthy, sensual, sensing, and emotional.

October 3, 1981

God always sees me and knows me. He knows my kind thoughts and feelings. He must also see my nastiness, my impurities, my anger, and sin.

Please, Father, see all of me and heal me.
Let me become integrated before you and in you. Please forgive me my sin. Joe.

I want to be holy, but not sure what that means for me today. My sexuality is not integrated. My power, my anger is not integrated. It seems as if my extroverted, intuitive aspect of my personality is very immature and "inferior." I need to integrate and don't know how.

October 17, 1981

My sexual life is still up in the air. I have never been celibate and have thought that it would be great to have a lover. However, that has never happened to me. So what have I done? I have gone to the bars or to the baths, and I would have to say mostly to the baths. They are not necessarily as awful as people say, and I have met some beautiful persons there. At the same time, they are not my ideal and, as time has gone on, have satisfied less and less. During this past year, however, there has been another movement, which is disconcerting somewhat: I am such a person of extremes. I love sex and the body and the earthiness of it all and can thoroughly enjoy them. I have been to the absolute bottom of the raunchy places in New York and have let myself go, so to speak.

At the same time, I also have another whole side to me that is contemplative and quiet. There has been growth in my spiritual life. I have meditated more this year and always found that when I had a good spiritual experience meditating (I would sometimes get "high" naturally) that I would want sex later on that day. I did an experiment with myself with that a few times and noticed how similar I would feel during a high after meditation and the high I would feel after orgasm with another person.

November 8, 1981

I sought psychotherapy to examine my sexuality, my feelings, and even to attempt to change my sexual orientation over a period of many years. I spent thousands of dollars in the process, only to realize that this is who I am. I sought spiritual direction from many sources and thoughtfully examined what God was asking of me. This process of self-discovery and self-examination was a painful and lengthy struggle, but, in the end, I stood before God and decided that, in this area, the teachings of the Catholic Church were wrong for me. I choose to dissent from the teachings in this area but that does not negate for me the Catholic faith and traditions, in which I believe and which I practice.

Unpublished Autobiography

1. An Order seminary (e.g., Franciscan or Dominican) prepares priests to serve in the Order's missions throughout the country or world. This is in contrast to a diocesan seminary, which prepares priests to serve in the local Church.
2. Reparative, or conversion, therapy assumes that homosexuality is a form of mental illness and therefore attempts to change a person's sexual orientation. Because the American Psychological Association and other mental health associations no longer categorize homosexuality as an illness, they have repudiated this type of therapy. Additionally, there is no solid evidence that individuals can change their orientation, and trying to do so can be psychologically harmful.
3. A specific bathhouse chain.

4. Natural law, the foundation of Catholic moral teaching on sexuality, claims that the purpose of human sexuality is to create life and therefore, homosexuality, masturbation, artificial contraception, and abortion all interfere with this process and are considered "intrinsically evil" and contrary to God's plan. Natural Law eliminates the possibility that for some individuals, it is natural to be sexually and emotionally attracted to members of the same sex.

5. Newman Centers provide spiritual support and religious services to Catholics attending non-Catholic colleges and universities. They are named after Cardinal John Henry Newman, who died in 1890. This Newman Center ministers to Catholic students at The Ohio State University.

6. DignityUSA is an organization of gay, lesbian, bisexual, and transgender Catholics that helps its members to affirm and integrate their sexuality and spiritually. It has local chapters throughout the United States and has been actively engaged in lobbying the Catholic bishops for a change of thinking about human sexuality.

7. Mass is the Catholic celebration of the Eucharist, a sacred meal of thanksgiving in memory of Jesus.

8. The lambda symbol (λ) was often used in the 1970s to identify gay men and lesbians.

9. Rudely Elegant was a popular gay dance bar in Columbus, Ohio.

10. Lauds is the morning prayer, and Compline is the night prayer that many Catholic religious communities recite or sing each day as part of the official prayer of the Church.

5

CHRIST IN MY LIFE

How God has taken care of me! He helped me to find Leo, who in a very deep and mystical way is Christ in my life. Others have also been Christ in my life, but now Leo is the main icon of Christ to me.
June 21, 2002

I met Leo during the fall of 1981, shortly after I had left another relationship. It was his first time at the monthly meeting of a gay men's support group, and I remember that I thought his name, Leo, was unusual. He was about my height, with light-brown hair and dark glasses, and I thought that he was nice-looking.

The next month, I arrived early for the meeting, and since he was the only other person there, we talked a little. I remember that he introduced himself to the group that night and told us that he was recently separated from his wife and had three small children. Whatever interest I had in Leo quickly left since I wasn't interested in children. In fact, I felt sorry that he was getting into the gay world with what I considered real "baggage." I was just breaking up from another relationship, was cynical and hurting at the time, and my attitude showed it.

I saw him at the next two meetings, and then somehow, we made a date for the day after Christmas.

Unpublished Autobiography

Leo and I had our first date on December 26. We obviously were not committed to each other, and I was still very afraid of commitment. I had planned to go to NYC and be in the Mineshaft, a "dark" bar-sex palace, on New Year's Eve. What happened, however, is that I spent the evening having dinner and talking to my confessor, who suggested that Leo was given to me by God and that I needed to open up and accept all. I decided not to go to the Mineshaft. I now truly believe I would have contracted HIV if I had gone and then I would have brought it back to Leo—a horrible thought. I thank God for his grace and the presence of my confessor that night.

January 1982

On a card sent to Leo:

My dear Leo,

I want you to see me and to know me because I want to be vulnerable before you. You are so good to me, so accepting, that I want to share with you. Thank you for being such a beautiful person. You are one of the best things that has happened to me!

Joe

January 17, 1982

I spent last evening at Leo's till he went to work. He fixed a big meal; we talked, and had sex twice. We had sex mostly to relieve my anxiety. I can't seem to be comfortable around him anymore. When I left, I went to the tubs and had sex again, and then, of course, I feel like shit. I feel that I'm not going to get through this, and if I don't, I intend to kill myself.

I've been through this before and never make it. Here I am, faced with a beautiful man, and I can't accept it. Maybe I really believe (deep down) that my mother is right, that I'm destined to be unhappy, that I am a schmuck. Why can't I feel towards him? He even said that he would try to make sex more exciting if he could. I want to cry as I write this because I want to break through whatever it is inside.

I feel that it's my last chance. God, I hate myself! I asked Leo for some space. I want to get through it and I don't think I can.

February 1982

I went on retreat to the Abbey of Gethsemani without Leo. When I got there, I unpacked and found the following note in my suitcase:

Dear Joe,

My prayers and thoughts are with you this weekend. Hope you have a great retreat.

My love, Leo.

When I returned, the following note was on the table, waiting for me:

Dear Joe,

Welcome Home! I missed you like you wouldn't believe. There's tuna salad in the fridge. Will call at lunch.

My love, Leo

My Leo is so good to me!

June 1983

In the past, I often used sexuality as a way to release my anger. I did not do this consciously but became aware that in my orgasm, I was getting in touch with anger. I met Leo and he was a very good person. Maybe I sensed that this man was to be important to me and so I didn't "close him off," but I have not been able to get in touch with my anger with him. The anger is associated somehow with raw sexuality—the dirtier, the more impersonal and raunchy, the better. With Leo there is goodness and gentleness, and I am not in touch with the other. Yet I find I still desire the "deeper" sexual experience—that pure animal, gut experience. I think that there has been much more integration since I met and formed a relationship with Leo. Don't know if there will be more integration. I know I want it. For now, I'll share it with my God, who sees and experiences me and who still loves me. I will try to stay open to my unconscious to see if s/he may want to "speak."

June 25, 1983

Last night was very interesting and important for me—at a level that I don't even want to analyze. My sister and her kids had come over to watch *East of Eden* on the video with Leo and me. We had all gone to the wedding of a woman who was the ex-wife of an old lover of mine. I know that I had been moved by the wedding, the commitment, and the faith, and also how I was afraid of that somehow. I don't know. I do know that I had been somewhat distant inside from Leo all day. The movie was quite emotional for me because it dealt with Cal's trying to be loved by his father even to the point of trying somehow to buy it. He couldn't and finally had to accept that. In the end, the father let his son know, in a small way, that he was loved. Somehow, that opened an area in me again. Later, after everyone else left, Leo and I began to become affectionate with each other.

When Leo and I began, however, I was at a place inside where I opened up. We really did make love last night and not just have sex. It took hours (felt that way, anyhow), and I was open. Several times we spoke, and I recorded it in my mind. We were listening to music at the time, a French record, and also a record titled *For Lovers* by Rod McKuen.

At one point during our lovemaking, I said to Leo, "Leo, thank you for loving me." He responded, "Thank you for letting me in." The tone was such that it sounded as if he has been trying to get in and not knowing how. Of course, he couldn't come in unless I opened the door. I have been doing that, but slowly and carefully. His words said so much because I have a terribly hard time allowing him or anybody else in close.

Later, the words of the record said, "I don't know what I'd do if you left or went away." I responded as if Leo had voiced those words, and I replied out loud, "I'd die." And then I thought of my writing at Gethsemani when I said that without the Eucharist, I would die. In my thoughts, I became aware of the fact that Leo is also Eucharist for me. Jesus is present to me in the Eucharist, and I adore him there and believe that he is there. We become one and I grow into him. Jesus is also present to me in Leo, and I adore him there, too. By becoming more involved in [Leo's] life and letting him into mine, we become more one. The paschal mystery happens again and new life rises. Both are Eucharist to me, and I "feed" on both lives. Together, we all become one.

As I held Leo in my arms, I began to pray, praising Jesus and the Father. I was one with all—with Leo and with God. I felt integrated and recalled how often I used to go to the river and pray—and get high praying—often ending in praising God verbally. Later on that day, maybe eight hours later, I would become aware that I wanted sexual release and I noticed that the orgasm was similar to the "high" of the morning. Last night, with Leo in my arms, I was "high" again, and I was praising God. (Maybe it wasn't a "high" but I was so much more attuned and aware of all sensations.) I seemed so much more integrated and whole.

As I laid there in awe of all that was happening, I heard the words inside in my thoughts, *Joseph, don't you see? You are becoming one with me.* I heard them as if Jesus was saying them to me. All is in him, and I am growing, letting go of my control, letting Leo in, and becoming one with my God. Slowly, the idea of being a monk is letting go inside. It is still a good life, and maybe someday, but not now, not with Leo in my life. I am to find myself and God in a physical intimate relationship, in relationship with Leo. God will come alive to me in relationships.

September 11, 1983

At this time in my life, Leo seems to be like a key that allows me access to deeper, inner rooms within. Maybe it isn't monasticism, per se, that I'm attracted to but a union, a oneness, a unity with the divine and with myself.

January 28, 1984

Leo and I were making love in the living room. We were lying in each other's arms, and I was very much aware of my senses. I reflected back to what my confessor had asked me before: "How will Leo fit in with your passionate needs? You have passion in prayer and in sex. Where is Leo in that?"

As I was reflecting on this, I went to another level and thought, *This is it. The answer doesn't lie in the extreme passion, but in the ordinary, in the common, in the day-to-day, in the loving acts of each moment.* I thought of St. Thérèse of Lisieux and her "little way" of sanctity[1] and could only say, "Yes." I felt a sense of well-being and oneness at that point.

March 3, 1984

As I sit in my room alone, at Gethsemani, saying the Rosary,[2] I am very quiet. I pray, "Help me to surrender to you," and then I thought, *How can I surrender to God when I can't even surrender to Leo's love?* I am also aware that Leo comes to mind very much this weekend—what he is doing, how he feels, and what he thinks. There is no great longing for him or pining for him, but I think of him, of how much he loves me and how I can be secure in his love, of how I can let go with him and be myself. What a good gift from God. What more can I ask?

I then went to chapel and I was alone. A monk was playing the organ, and the music filled the church. As I sat there, I thought of Leo. I felt calm. I was aware of prayer, of being moved, of yearning for oneness with Jesus. I was also aware that Leo was there in that union. I want both, and yet maybe I can't have union with God without learning how to be intimate with Leo. I saw [Leo] in my mind and I smothered Leo with hugs and kisses. I feel like I'm at a place where I want to make sure Leo is there for me, but I have trouble committing myself to being there for him.

I have been there for him in some ways, too. I am sexually faithful with Leo, and I think I am slowly letting my life be adapted in relationship to him. I am certainly going much slower and with more ambivalence and struggle than Leo is with me.

Dear God, please don't let me lose him.
Please help me to open up to him before he goes.

September 22, 1984

Today I was driving in my car, reflecting on Leo and God. I'm not sure who was first. I remembered making love with Leo last night and reflecting what a good man he is. I felt humbled before God that here I am, a man with a promiscuous past, meeting another man, a virgin in the gay world, who has similar values and hopes and who absolutely loves me. I then reflected on this God, this force at the center of the universe, who is total love. For a second or so, I experienced the love of this Being, and intertwined was my thankfulness for bringing me to Leo. My body tingled all over as I gave thanks.

January 12, 1985

It seems clear to me that Leo has been good for me in my life. Because of him, I have slowly allowed my wall of self-protection, of insulation to come down (and not without a constant fight!). To allow him to love me brings joy, but it also is frightening and difficult. It forces me to depend upon someone else, to open myself to the risk of rejection, of failure, of pain. Without it, though, I run the risk of closure and self-absorption and death.

March 3, 1985

Leo and I moved into our new home in May of this year, and it is home for both of us. That was a big step for me—more of a good-bye to my monastic-life fantasy and more of a commitment to my life with Leo. Since then, I have made my will and declared legally that Leo Radel is my partner in life. He is to be given my possessions and my life. In reality, that was and is a big step for me. I really have come a long way in my journey through life, and I feel that I am more whole (and maybe more holy) than I ever was in the past. I hope that I continue to grow, and I truly pray that Leo and I grow closer together.

December 13, 1985

It is Christmas Day in my new home with Leo—really our new home—and that is good.

I thank you, Father,
for peace in my life now after so many years.
I am with Leo, who loves me. I have a job. I am at peace in Leo and my new
home.
Keep us safe, healthy, and faithful,
and let Christmas 1986 be one which finds our family unbroken.
Joe

December 25, 1985

Leo and I drove down to Gethsemani for a retreat. The ride down was interesting. Leo took a nap, and every so often, I'd look over at him and realize how much I love him. He is mine (and I am his) to share—his

76

body, his gentle soul, his personality. How good God has been to me in giving me someone who loves me, and someone I love.

Thank you, God, for your gift.

June 5, 1987

Dear Leo,

Six years ago tonight, we went out for dinner. We both exchanged flowers and both wore suits. You were very much in love then, and I was scared to death. When I think of all my mixed messages ("come closer, go away"), I cringe inside because it must have been difficult for you. I was very "crispy" and terribly afraid that I would break apart if I let you get too close. Even when you moved in, I would put some distance between us with talk of the monastery or say, "This just isn't going to work," or "Well, if you and I make it." How did you ever deal with it? What kept you there with me?

What kept me staying with you? What kept me wanting more with you even when we had to deal with money problems and your terrible work schedule? Can you remember—we had 4 days and nights together every month!

It is six years later and we are still together, living in a nice home, and "making it." We still are trying to make our relationship better, but we know that what we have is good.

When I think back over my life, I don't know how I made it before you. You have become part of my life: we are separate and yet we are one. With my breath, with my life, I love you, Leo Radel, and I ask God's choicest blessings upon you and us.

Love, Joe

Valentine's Day 1988

I cannot get over the fact that Leo Radel loves me as I am, good points and bad points. I used to believe that no one would ever come along in my life, and I am afraid he will disappear with the morning sun. But God brought Leo into my life to help me to experience love and to give me an opportunity to love someone else. Leo was the perfect gift. He and I are similar in some ways, and this gives us common values and beliefs to share. We are different, too, in our response to life, others, and the world. This helps me to accept myself—my eccentricities and hyperness—because Leo accepts these in me and still loves me. So maybe I can accept it, too. I also try to accept his tarnished points, too.

I am in a gay and committed relationship, and I was thinking this morning in the car that this seems to be my vocation in the world. Being gay in this committed relationship is the way I am being called to holiness.

September 13, 1988

In February of this year, Leo and I gave a presentation on intimacy in our relationship to the Newman Center's Gay Men's Support Group. When Leo and I do these talks, it helps to uplift me (us). For me, I get in touch again with the goodness of this relationship. It really does seem to be a good one.

March 1, 1989

Today, I sat next to a coworker who was at my Commissioners' Award luncheon. She really liked Leo and talked about what a nice man he is, how compassionate and handsome. She wondered how we ever met, since she didn't think I would be attracted to him because he is so quiet. It reaffirmed to me how sweet Leo is and how fortunate I am to have him in my life. I am still insecure in that I hate to think of him leaving me or falling in love with someone else. Last night, he introduced a new sexual practice that he wants, and I wondered if he is getting tired of what we have been doing. I guess that, even if he is, it does not mean that he is tired of me!

July 26, 1989

Well, I've crossed the line in faithfulness with Leo. I've soiled the white garment for the first time since I committed to him on November 12, 1982. I touched another man at the spa. I was in the shower and I was cruising. There was another man there, and I got an erection and waited to see if he did. Once I knew he was interested, I carried it on a bit but then got frightened because I didn't want to carry it out fully with him. I turned around and finished my shower, left, and began to dry off. He followed me out and stood right in front of me. I was then overwhelmed with lust or excitement. I touched his penis, and I immediately pulled back and got out. I felt bad.

I told Leo, and he seemed to handle it fine. He told me that if I had told him that I was seeing someone else and wanted out of the relationship, then he would be hurt. This did not threaten him. I told him that I had learned something about myself, and he asked what. I told him that I had learned that I can't play with fire and [that] cruising is playing with fire. This is especially so when I am under a lot of stress and I am vulnerable. I also learned that I stopped the cruising and the touch because of my bond with Leo and that this is important to me.

March 11, 1990

Early on in our relationship I was sexually dysfunctional because I couldn't have sex completely without getting in touch with this rawness/

78

anger. Leo didn't make me angry and was not just a trick. He was a person of gentleness, kindness, and caring. Over time, my therapist helped me to get through my blockage and learn to experience sexual expression with gentleness, caring, and intimacy.

July 11, 1990

My birthday is over and I am 42 years old. Such is life. Leo took me out to dinner and sent me 24 white carnations with baby's breath and greenery at the office. Both were appreciated. Oh, he also said that I had $50.00 to spend when I wanted to buy some leather, but I won't hold him to that since he doesn't have the money. I frankly don't know how he will pay for the flowers at this point. Anyhow, his comment to me was "You're worth it." Nice. He really does love me. I was thinking of that last night when I cuddled next to him in the bed. He was asleep, and I just thanked God for Leo in my life.

August 26, 1990

Today is the ninth anniversary of my first date with Leo. God, it is hard to believe that I have known him that long, and truly a grace that I have stayed with him, with anyone, that long. He worked last night, and I leave for work before he comes home in the morning, so I left him a card.

Dear Leo,

Nine years ago today we had our first "date" at your apartment. You started me on a journey that brought so many surprises. Because of you, I learned to become intimate. I learned that I can love and that I can be loved. Because of you, my family reconciled with me. You are truly a grace and gift.

Thanks for our first date and all the years since. May they continue.

Love, Me

December 26, 1990

We had a surprise party for my mother's 80th birthday. Leo was there with all the rest of the people, and they could think whatever they wanted. Neither Dad nor Mom seemed embarrassed. At one point I had my feet up on the chair Leo was sitting in. Later, I moved, and the old lady from across the street looked at Leo and rather loudly asked who he was. He told her his name and said that he was a friend of mine and of my sister. She waited a few seconds or so and then, again in a voice that could be heard, "Well, by the way he had his feet on your chair, I thought he was more than a friend."

March 19, 1991

Today is our anniversary of commitment. On November 12, 1982, Leo and I committed to each other. It wasn't a wonderful romantic time with a big affair. No, it was the end of our agreement with our therapist to stay together no matter what during the previous six months. Leo and I both knew that I was having trouble with commitment and intimacy. Even though we had lived together for several months, I still had sex in the book-stores at times, and, of course, I would always tell Leo. Just a few days before the end of the agreement period, I had done this again and I told him. I don't remember exactly what his reaction was, but I know I told him in the car, and I think he was dropping me off at work.

I knew from his reaction that I was going to have to make a decision. I also had the gut reaction that if I said I wasn't ready and wanted an exten-sion of the agreement, Leo was going to say "no," and would begin to date. I was determined not to lose him because I also knew, even though I was afraid of intimacy and commitment, that he was the best thing that had ever happened to me and that he was from God. I truly believed that in spite of my fear. The agreement ended, and I committed to him. He accepted and basically renewed the commitment that he had made earlier. We count as our anniversary the day when we first met in 1981 and decided to start our life together. This is a good relationship, and I am thankful to God for giving me the grace of Leo and for helping me get through my own emotional blocks fearing intimacy. Without that, I would be lost!

November 11, 1991

Leo and I had a major fight this week over his buying his new car and the terrible expense over it. We fought, and I was really mad; I think he was hurt. I thought about it all for a day and wrote him an apology even though I have some real doubts that I was so at fault. It just doesn't seem worth it to get angry at him—it only upsets both of us and he doesn't see my point of view. So, this is just the way it is. This is the letter I wrote him:

Dear Leo,
I have spent the entire day thinking of little else than the fight last night. I wanted to understand why I was so mad last night and why you were so pissed off, too. I replayed your comment that you felt that you had a right to be upset with my comment or attitude that you should be happy you are with me. When I asked you to explain, you said that you felt devalued and that I was "taking care" of you. I made you feel put down and second-class. I put myself in your place today and realized how that must have sounded; it probably sounded terrible. I am sorry.

I know that you love me very much, and I also realize that you give a great deal to this relationship (some might think you give more than your share). I do value your part in this relationship and I know how much you do give. I guess I'm asking you to put yourself in my place a little, too. You know how I worry about money and meeting the budget. I know that this is all unimportant to you, or so it seems to me—whenever I try to talk about money, you toss it off and say that it is not important.

Then I feel devalued and I can't talk to you about it. I feel very stressed right now, and, unfortunately, I'm not like most of mankind who feels better after they spent some money shopping; it only freaks me out more. When the dishwasher went out and I priced them at the store, I got panicky. I had to cash in most of my savings bonds for the refrigerator, and all I see is money going out the door. So with it all, I was stressed, and I guess last night, I just wished that you hadn't spent so much money for the car.

I try my best to keep a budget, and I was worried about the car payment and the extra insurance money. Instead of coming out and saying that (I'm afraid to talk money to you for the reasons above), I deflected it and was passive-aggressive. I am sorry about that—I really am. Part of it was my frustration. I guess I don't feel that my contribution to the relationship in terms of the budget or saving money for vacations is even appreciated.

You may appreciate it, I don't know. I only know that I get the feeling at times that you think it is a joke, and then I feel really discounted. That is something that I bring to the relationship, and I got the feeling that it didn't even matter to you. I think that it came out last night. I know that I reacted to your getting pissed and that it made me even madder. I truly love you and don't want to hurt you. I am sorry if I did. Can't we make up?

Love, Me

We made up and both apologized to each other. I felt better even if I also feel that I gave too much ground. We all compromise in life. That is the way it is.

November 22, 1992

I got a nice card from Leo a few days or so ago for no particular reason.

When we first started out, my feelings for you were so intense that, at times, I was overwhelmed by the joy and the thrill of falling in love. I never thought I could love you any more than I did then. Through the years, we've changed and grown in many ways, separately and together, and our love has changed and grown right along with us. Yet in some ways, nothing has changed at all. I look at you now and I fall in love all over again.

Love, Leo

March 19, 1993

My abandonment fears are very high. Leo has met a man at the Post Office[3] with whom he has lunch every Tuesday. Leo also invited him to our "chef" party this past Wednesday. Leo hugged him, and I was jealous. Leo says that there is nothing there, but my feelings are still the same. Interestingly, at the spa yesterday afternoon, I envisioned Leo telling me someday that he was in love with someone else and that our relationship was over. I said to him in my fantasy, "Well, I knew that this day would come. I just never knew when." And then I had to decide what I was going to do with the rest of my life.

July 2, 1993

We had sex the other night, and I am still having trouble with that. Part of me isn't attracted anymore, and I hope that isn't permanent. I have trouble with my erections and worry about that, too. Is it the medicine? Is it my age? Is it my lack of desire? I do love Leo and I want to keep him in my life.

January 23, 1994

Father, help me to find peace.
Help me to deal with (accept) my homosexuality, my active relationship with
Leo.
Help me to finally (again) come to peace with who I am.
Do I always have to walk this same road over, time and again?
I want to trust you, my God. I want to freely place myself, body and soul, mind
and emotions, into your care.
Above all else, Father, I want to be with you for all eternity.
And, frankly, Lord, I'm not even sure of what this entails.
I have so many conflicting emotions and thoughts and beliefs.
Please, take me as I am—confused and torn and afraid—and carry me in your
arms.
Please love away this mess I find myself in and make sure that, at my death, I
will wake up in you,
my Lord and my God. Jesus, I trust in you.
Amen.

January 24, 1994

Have been thinking of my relationship with Leo all day. We had sex last night. I learned one thing—I still do love Leo. I enjoyed being with him, smelling him and kissing him, but the excitement, the passion, is not there. Oh, we had sex, but my erection was not strong and my interests were not there. It just doesn't excite me anymore with Leo.

That panics me inside because I think that this means the relationship is over. I know other gay couples that don't have sex anymore, and I always said that ours wouldn't suffer that problem. And, then, here I am. After orgasm, Leo and I just lay in each other's arms. That was fine. I apologized to Leo that I was a mess, and he said I wasn't. He was very supportive. He seemed to enjoy it. What is wrong with me? Is this the depression?

Please, Lord, help me out.
Please help me to get through this, too.
I want to be faithful to Leo, and I want to have my own insides satisfied.
Father, please!

February 10, 1994

Sex is less important in my life but still important. I guess I'm not "into it" as much as Leo, and I pray that my passion for and with Leo will come back stronger. I'm very glad I'm with him; don't know how I'd be without him. Others are envious of our relationship. Leo and I will go through a recommitment ceremony now that Mom and Dad have passed. Still hard to believe they are gone.

May 27, 1994

Our vacation was okay but not wonderful. I am sick and don't know what is wrong. I've had intestinal problems even before we left for NYC, and it hasn't gotten any better. Leo and I only had sex twice in all that time, and it wasn't very good. I'm just not with it, and then I worry that our relationship is over. That would be so sad. I wonder if I'm not scared of a deeper intimacy because of our talk of recommitment. I don't know.

July 3, 1994

After so many years, Lord, familiarity takes over
and it is somewhat more difficult to be so emotionally vulnerable
as we were in the beginning.
And yet, it was good to be with Leo in a comfortable manner.
As I touched him, I realized how ordinary it is and yet,
that is exactly as it is supposed to be.
Life is ordinary, and you are there in the ordinariness of life.
As I held Leo, I was aware that this man truly loves me and I truly love him.
Thank you.
The body, Lord, is so beautiful and good,
and it has been so distorted by religion through the years.

I sometimes wonder if Christians are really aware of the significance
of the Incarnation.
God became flesh so that we could see him and feel him.
It is only through our bodies that we can convey our feelings and spirits.
Help me to experience you in my life now and for all eternity in the next.
Amen.

December 24, 1995

Father,
today is the first day of the New Year, 1996.
Help both Leo and me to grow together and more deeply.
Help us to rekindle our love and passion and to keep us faithful to each other.
I do believe that we are supposed to be together
and 1996 will hopefully see us recommit to each other in a public ceremony.
Help us to be a witness to others of the possibility of a long-term relationship.
Help us to bring others to you through our witness.
Into your hands, Father, I place my destiny and my being.
Amen.

January 1, 1996

If I don't believe, at a very deep level, that gay is good, then facing God when I die is frightening because I'm afraid of being rejected and going to hell. In fact, I'm not trusting God as all good and as really being there for me. I am not trusting myself and my experience of gayness in my life and its importance in helping me to love another person. With that going on, it is not surprising that I am afraid to recommit to Leo in a public ceremony because I am actually stating then to myself and others that I want to be in a gay relationship and that this is truly who I am before myself, others, and my God.

At a very deep level, I am facing it again in a truly existential point in my life (middle age and that crisis) and saying that this is who I am and that I will be living and dying as a Catholic gay man. With my ambivalence morally with gayness, it is not surprising that I am afraid of the recommitment and of dying into a God that I am projecting and transferring my fears of rejection onto. It all makes sense intellectually, and I'm sure that I am correct in my assumptions and analysis. What I haven't done now is to go the next step and actually go through the barrier. I am much closer to that leap of faith than before, and I'm sure I'll do it.

February 20, 1996

Last night with Leo in my arms, I was comfortable with him, I wanted him close to me, and I acknowledged how good he is for me. I think I've gone to a deeper level of intimacy with myself and God, and maybe even with Leo (obviously), and I'm afraid. It is funny to me because at work, where I have his picture on my desk, I'll sometimes look at it during the day and say, "I love you, Leo." I do love him but am afraid of the intimacy, to tell him.

Last night as we lay there, I asked Leo if he loved me, and he said, with meaning, "Yes, I love you." I asked him why, and he immediately responded, "Because of your innate goodness." Wow! I wasn't expecting that answer, denied it only to have him reaffirm it. I told him how good he is for me and kissed him. Last night I kept thinking, *This is where it all is, Joe—in the ordinary. Holiness is in the ordinary, in my life with Leo.*

February 26, 1996

Help me, Lord, to be truly thankful for my sexuality.
When Leo and I make love and when I am totally present to it,
I know Leo loves me.
He is your love for me made incarnational.
Leo's touch of my body, of me, soothes my hunger to be touched—
my skin hunger—
and it soothes my soul also.

I am thankful that I am in a relationship of such depth. Leo truly loves me, and in spite of my ambiguities and doubts, I love him. We like each other. I like his physical looks and find him attractive. I like his personality—his kindness and gentleness. He is considerate of my feelings. I like his outlook on life—his optimism and joyfulness. Leo gives me a way to love, to express myself, to get out of myself.

I am thankful that Leo is spiritual and is Catholic. My Catholicism runs deep and is a part of me. While Leo may have different views, images, and words, he shares the fundamentals with me. He values the Eucharist, sharing the Body and Blood[4] of Christ with me and with the world. We are united, not only in the flesh but also in the Spirit. This is very important to me and helps this relationship succeed.

May 25, 1996

I was sitting at my desk at the Abbey of Gethsemani, reading a few pages from *Sacrament of Sexuality*, by Morton and Barbara Kelsey, and then reflecting on them. I must have been thinking of me and God, because I decided to do an experiment of having a conversation with God. I decided just to put my pen to the paper and let it write what it wanted. This is what I wrote:

Me: Lord, you know me through and through—who I am and why I am. You know I worry about my relationship with Leo, about my lack or lessening of passion, about my attraction to others at times, about my attraction to the idea of being a monk. What am I to do? You know I often doubt whether you truly love me as gay, as sexual, as earthy.

God: Joseph, I love you with every fiber of my being. I love you whether you are gay or straight, black or white, good or bad. You are precious to me, and I'll never let you down, no matter what. Life is life, and in the midst of your problems and questions, I am here with you.

Joseph, years ago, you asked me what you were to do with Leo and with the idea of being a monk. In both cases I gave you an answer. Remember and relive it. I told you, "Find me in Leo," and I also told you, "I will make you holy in the world." Both answers, my son, are still valid. You have what many others desire—a true relationship that is based on love and affection. Leo loves you and is faithful to you. You also love Leo, despite all your fears and ambiguities.

You are not a celibate, Joseph, and I didn't ordain you to be. Stop worrying about a lifestyle that isn't yours. Again I ask you, "How many have what you have?" Not many. Grow together with Leo. Develop each other's strengths and forgive each other's weaknesses. I live in him, Joseph, and I live in you, too. I bless your relationship, and I have ordained it to be a vehicle for your salvation, wholeness, and growth.

I have also given you a contemplative bent to your personality, indeed to your very spirituality. That is one reason you are so attracted to the monastic life, and yet, I have not called you to live that lifestyle in a monastery. Trust me, Joseph, as I love you and only want the best for you. Visit Gethsemani, love it, draw grace from it, and then leave it to return to Leo and to the world of people and projects and ideas. There, my dear son, you will find me, and together we will re-create the world. I love you, and I will love you for all eternity.

Me: I want you. For all eternity, I want you.

God: You have me, and you will have me for all eternity, my child.

Me: Help me to be who you want me to be.

God: You are.

May 25, 1996

Leo and I were intimate, and we did something we don't usually do: after sex, we talked to each other. Leo said I started it with all the reasons he shouldn't love me: I'm fat and older. He came back with all the reasons he does love me, and I did that for him. It was nice. Interestingly, however, I held him and said, "I think I love you, Leo." With a lilt in his voice and a smile, he responded, "You think, huh?" He takes my intimacy fears and just blows them away, doesn't get threatened, and that is so helpful to me.

July 29, 1996

I was dancing and looking at Leo. I then closed my eyes while dancing (the way I usually dance), thinking of how wonderful he is for me and to me. At one point, I thought, *I think I'm falling in love with Leo all over again.* I went over and kissed him right there.

I thought of that last night. I had been in Cleveland for a conference and thought it would be nice to have sex when I got home. Leo was up for it. Well, I must have been really into it, because it was spectacular! Afterwards, we just lay in each other's arms and listened to music, each with our own thoughts. One of the thoughts that I had again was *I think I'm connecting or falling in love with Leo again.* It is such a neat feeling, but I really don't think I'm falling in love again. I just know that I am committed to him. What a journey!

October 5, 1996

Was watching TV with Leo last night, and he was flipping through the channels. He got a religious station talking about a new book, *The Great Delusion: Confronting Gay Christians.* The person who wrote it said that no matter what gay Christians feel for each other or think about their relationship with God, homosexuality is forbidden. To think otherwise is a delusion, and, although they did not say it in the short time I listened, it would put us at moral peril. Leo flipped it off, and I said, "Thank you." But my mind began tripping over it and I immediately began to feel panic. *What if they are right? I'm going to hell.* It raised all my doubts right under the surface. I told Leo, and he was surprised. I asked him if he had doubts, and he said "no," then continued. "Joe, it is a gift, a charism," to which I said, "What is a gift?" Leo answered, "Homosexuality." I asked, "How is it a gift?" Leo said, "Joe, it is a gift that I can love another man. I don't know why this is so, but it is, and I just accept it." My reaction was, *God, why do I torture myself and Leo just trusts?*

October 9, 1996

My emotions are pretty dry, and I'm afraid of the future. I am starting to get scared about the ceremony. Is it really going to happen? How will I get through it all? I am starting to think, *What if they are right? What am I recommitting to?* But I will not give in to that temptation.

October 14, 1996

I am beginning to get really nervous and yet, at the same time, I know I'm all right and in control. This afternoon, Leo and I were intimate and I had some erection difficulty. I'm not really surprised and didn't kill myself over it. I was thinking of the ceremony. Nothing like stacking the deck against my sexual functioning (ha!). We did have our orgasm, but the important thing is that I tried to be present in the now with Leo. I am recommitting my life to him, and I remember saying, as I had my orgasm, something like "I am giving you everything. I am scared to death, but I am doing it."

Later, when we were hugging, I asked him if he was nervous about tomorrow, and he shook his head right and left, saying, "No, I'm not really nervous. I'm sure." I took that to mean he has no doubts about being with me. I don't either, really. I just know that this is a very important decision for me spiritually and emotionally. My "fundamental option,"[4] as spoken about in moral theology, doesn't correspond to the Church's. Maybe that is my vocation, to push the barriers in this century. Who knows? I know that my "option" or stance in my existential life is still directed to God; at least I want it there. I want God above everything, and I will probably find him as the Other, but I will also need to recognize that I will find him in Leo, in myself, and in our relationship.

Dear God, don't lose me (please).

November 8, 1996

The recommitment ceremony was a very spiritually and emotionally moving experience for everyone there. There were so many who said that it was the most beautiful "wedding" service or ceremony that they had ever attended. It was a very spiritually and emotionally moving experience for Leo and me, too!

November 10, 1996

Still haven't written about the ceremony. There are many thank-you notes to write, and we are back to work. Last night, Leo and I were intimate and afterwards just laid in each other's arms. I was somewhat distracted and "not there," and yet a part of me was very much there and I

88

reflected that this is my life now. I am living it. Thinking about that again got me in touch with what people said at the ceremony: Joe and Leo are role models—the goodness of our lives and relationship—fifteen years is a long time for a gay relationship.

I reflected that I am living now what I had hoped and prayed to have for so many years. I truly am in a good relationship that is wholesome, gay, physical, and spiritual. I am in a relationship with another Catholic, who values/accepts my beliefs and yet helps me not to go overboard and mess my mind up too much with my old religious tapes. Lying there, I thanked God for all his graces. I am amazed and humbled.

November 19, 1996

Jesus gave me this overwhelming and affirming recommitment ceremony as a sign of his love and approval. I do not mock the Church; I love it, and yet I call it to go further.

November 26, 1996

As Leo and I were dancing on New Year's Eve, Leo got really warm. He took his shirt off and then put his leather vest back on. He's gained some weight and has a little paunch. I looked at his paunch and loved it all. I liked my response.

At the stroke of midnight when they played the typical slow dance, I held Leo and invited Jesus to be with us. I became aware that Jesus was with Leo and me. He was part of us as a threesome. As I reflected on that, I then realized that Jesus was in Leo and Jesus was in me. So the union between the three of us was even more profound.

January 2, 1997

Last Thursday, I came home from work and masturbated. Later, after Leo had been home for a while, he came in naked with that devilish look in his eye. I told him that I had already "done the deed." He looked disappointed, and I felt disappointed. I told him to take his bath anyway; we'd do something.

Well, what I found that night was this: with my orgasm not an issue, I could concentrate on Leo's pleasure. It was neat, and I think I was more sensual than I usually am.

August 5, 1997

A gay couple, who are friends of ours, called to say that they were having trouble in their relationship and would like to talk to us. They came over and said that they believed that gay couples in trouble should talk to other gay couples about the problems. They were not looking for counseling but just honest interaction. So they told us their problems, and in trying to help them, we revealed our own difficulties in the past. We talked for three hours, and they said that it was helpful if only to discover that other couples have similar problems sometimes. (We all think that our problems are unique.)

Right before they left, one of them asked what kept us together during our difficult times. We looked at each other, and I went first. I said that I had decided that Leo was so good that I would not let him out of my life. The thing was that I choked up trying to say it aloud. Leo said something similar about who I am and that he wanted to continue to know that. It revealed to me how bonded I am to Leo.

We were surprised that they chose us (honored, really), since they are friends with another couple they've known longer than Leo and me. The answer they gave us was that we had been in relationship for 15 years and doing well and they trusted us. What an honor and compliment.

August 23, 1997

Last evening, a close friend came over for dinner and we had a nice time. After dinner, we were sitting around at the table talking and having an after-dinner drink. Somehow, we got talking about relationships and I mentioned that my ambivalent feelings and inner conflicts I had in the beginning stages of my relationship with Leo had been so difficult for him the first year and even into some of the other "first" years. Before I committed to Leo on November 12, 1982, I was still not totally faithful sexually. After the commitment I was, but I also was sexually dysfunctional and so afraid of intimacy even though I had committed to Leo after the first year. I mentioned that I didn't know how Leo handled it.

Leo almost put a reason or excuse for my "unfaithfulness" by saying "but that was your pattern." I don't know if my friend said something then, but ultimately, Leo just said, "But I got the Grand Prize." Emotionally, I just reached out to him after that comment and thanked God. I really didn't react much at the time except that I did say, "That's sweet." I thought about it much later.

July 8, 1998

This has been an interesting time for me with Leo's children. Last weekend, we celebrated Leo's 49th birthday, and his children were all here on Sunday. They took *both* of us to breakfast and then we spent the day together. I was more relaxed with them and just was myself. They seemed relaxed also. It was a nice day.

July 11, 1999

Leo and I have been talking more and touching more. That is one thing that I really missed when we were fighting and arguing—the lack of physically touching Leo and our emotional closeness. By physical touching I don't mean sex but just holding hands and being close physically. We do that a lot, and I really noticed its absence and my reaction to that. I am bonded to him.

September 18, 1999

Leo and I were intimate. At the beginning, I thought about God loving me when Leo loves me, and my loving God when I love Leo. In a sense, when I love Leo in his physicality, I am in some sense loving God at the same time. It was a beautiful thought, and I intended to love Leo as the best lover I could. But it didn't happen that way in reality. I became selfish and really got off on Leo taking care of me. I didn't do that totally (I was not all selfish) but more than maybe I should have. At the same time, I remember stopping in the middle and asking him if he was enjoying taking care of me. He said yes, so what could I do? Afterwards, I concentrated on Leo and he seemed really pleased and satisfied.

I wonder if one of the reasons I had difficulty accepting this is because I hit another layer of "I don't deserve to think about my pleasure, to just let go and take it." Maybe not; I am confused. Anyway, I want sometime to concentrate on him, but, in reality, I then take care of me first. I wish I were less selfish.

January 30, 2000

Sex is going to be different from now on, and we are entering another phase. I just have to get through the transition. Sex with Leo is not going to be new and exciting after almost 19 years. God, 19 years—who would have ever thought that I, with my background, would ever be in a relationship of so many years! This is pure grace from God with my cooperation with his grace. That, I do believe without a doubt.

April 23, 2000

Leo is in my life. How we met was almost an accident. He was not my "type," and I learned that I was not his either, and yet here we are. I didn't trust Leo (or anyone else, for that matter) and so tested Leo during those first few years, yet he didn't leave. I didn't like children and didn't want to deal with an ex-wife, yet I didn't leave, either. I don't like our different views of money and budgeting. We have been through so much over the years, and yet even last night, we cuddled on the loveseat-recliner as we watched television. It is rare that we don't touch each other or kiss at least once a day. We have a good relationship.

Without Leo, I would not be alive, or, if I was, I would not be any happier inside. Leo has helped me to accept and to trust myself because he truly loves me. Years ago, God told me that when I loved Leo and received love from him, I also loved God and God loved me in return. Leo has helped me to accept more deeply that I am lovable, that he loves me, and that God also loves me. Several years ago, God also told me that while I wanted God a lot, God wanted me even more. I can accept that as true. Leo leads me to God, and hopefully, I do the same for him.

I am utterly amazed at what I am writing. It seems so different than I normally think or feel, and yet, right now, it is true and I accept it as true. I accept myself as I am, inadequacies and grace together.

December 12, 2000

On Friday night, Leo and I were intimate. As I held him in my arms and made love to him, I was very aware of our bodies and of the holiness of our loving. I asked God into the mix. Later as I reflected on this, I also affirmed the goodness of the earthiness and messiness of sex. God made us flesh. He embodied us and made us sexual. Our lovemaking, using genital sexuality, can only be what it is, and that is messy sometimes, earthy, sensual, and above all, holy.

Thank you, Father, for your gifts to me, your grace in my life.
Thank you for my body and its earthiness; thank you for my deep spirituality.
Continue to draw me to yourself so that when I die,
I will die right into your arms, your life.
For all eternity, I want to be with you.

May 13, 2002

This Sunday, *The Columbus Dispatch* will be announcing our 21st anniversary in the paper in their new section for same-sex unions and anniversaries. We will have our picture there also. Should prove interesting, and we are excited. Can't really believe *The Dispatch* is doing this, but it is wonderful. I sent an e-mail to some people telling them about it.

November 13, 2002

A few years early we purchased our 25th anniversary rings while in St. Bart[5]. These are the real Cartier's original unity rings. They are three rings interconnecting. I think of them as a trinity of sorts—Leo, me, and God—all interconnected in relationship.

March 9, 2003

Had an interesting experience the other afternoon. I was walking to the jewelry store to have them polish my new ring and buff out a scratch on top. As I was walking down the street, there was a young man who was sitting on the brick low fence in front of the high-rise building for seniors. He smiled at me, and I acknowledged him. There was a sexual interaction that I felt. I walked on to the jewelry store, and I think I looked back at one point. He was looking at me.

When I finished my business at the store, I began to walk up the street towards that young man. Instead of walking on the same side of the street, however, I walked across the street at the light and so was on the opposite side of the street when I passed him. At some level, I had debated at that light deciding to walk across the street instead of right past him.

As I walked down the street, he smiled at me from across the street, and I returned it. When I got into my car, I had to pass him again and he smiled again. I knew that I could have easily picked him up because he made some motions to that effect. He may have been a hustler or just a horny young man. As I drove on, I could feel that tension in my body and was aware that years ago, I would have picked him up.

This temptation was the first that I have felt or experienced in years and, in some ways, reminded me of my days in New York City or even in Columbus in the '70s. As I drove on, I was glad it passed. I looked at and felt my trinity wedding ring and realized again how bonded I am to Leo. I also realized that I had made decisions at several points during the entire experience not to jeopardize my faithfulness to Leo. I thanked God for helping me not be too terribly tempted.

April 18, 2003

This past week, I had two experiences that were the same but powerful. I was sitting at my desk and looked up at the picture I have on my desk of Leo holding me as we sat at the top of a mountain in Colorado—our vacation several years ago after a Dignity convention. I looked at Leo in the picture and could not help but feel a wave of love for him, even saying to myself aloud, "Leo, I so love you." My eyes teared up.

Thank you, God, for the gift of Leo in my life.
How did you know I needed him so much?

Well, I guess I can answer that one—
it is so obvious that I was a mess before him.
Thank you, Father, again.

June 13, 2003

Last evening, Leo and I were sitting in the loveseat-recliner, watching television. As we do every time we sit in this chair, we held hands. For some reason, the last two fingers on my right hand were tingling and hurting. For about ten minutes, we didn't touch at all and I found myself really missing it. We found another way of holding hands. Touch—oh, how holy is this sense. How incarnational that I am "touched" in my soul by the simple act of being touched and touching.

Thank you, Father, for this wonderful gift.
Thank you for Leo's life in mine and mine in his, and yours in ours!

January 26, 2004

My relationship with Leo is strong. We deal with problems and don't let things fester too much without seeking professional help. We are not broke. We have room to grow and develop our strengths and forgive each other our areas of weakness and fear. We do try to accept ourselves and each other as we are.

April 30, 2004

At church this past Sunday, Leo and I saw the couple we had helped a few months ago, and one of them came up, looked us in the eyes, stumbled around for what he wanted to say, and then just started. I blocked some of it out (probably because it was so positive), but I remember him saying that he has known us from the Gay Parents' group in the early '80s. He said that he has always carried us in his heart, not because of the birthday and anniversary cards we send, not because of what we do for the gay cause, not because of my letters to the editors in the local secular and religious papers, not because we helped them by counseling them in their relationship, but just because "there was always Joe and Leo." He said that he loved us in his heart. Both Leo and I were just stunned listening to him tell us his deeply held feelings.

May 16, 2004

After being intimate with Leo, I reflected on the awesomeness of sexual communication and realized that it is a language all its own. The touching of

94

skin, the warmth of our bodies, the smell of each other, and the vulnerability of our beings all speak the language. Part of this sexual communication is very much physical and takes us outside ourselves in a way. Some would call this the "animal" instinct and denigrate it. I think that is misguided. We humans are made of bodies that seek their own pleasure, but there is more. In sexual activity, we are able to express our emotions, both positive and negative. In sexual activity, we can also express friendship, affection, and love.

I believe that sexual communication in a committed relationship expresses the unitive aspect of sexual expression. The Church allows this with heterosexuals in marriage but also insists that their sexual activity be open to the transmission of life. I believe that gays can express their love with the resulting unitive aspect. Gays may not be "creative" in producing offspring, but look at how many gays are creative—art, music, floral arrangements, interior decorating, doctors, nurses, social welfare, counseling, and on and on.

December 16, 2004

Fr. John McNeill told me that there is a new book coming out entitled *Sons of the Church: The Witness of Gay Catholic Men*, by Thomas R. Stevenson, PhD. John said that Leo and my stories are there, and as with all the other interviews, we reached a point where our relationship with God became more of an authority in our lives than our relationship with the Church. This is a real insight that I had never thought of directly, even though I'm sure I have heard it before and probably from John. Now that I have heard it again, it does ring true to my experience. It is not that I totally discount what the official Church teaches, but it is filtered with my own experience and my own relationship with God. Regarding the book— I do remember giving an interview to someone years ago but can't remember when. I think it was after my parents had died.

November 8, 2005

Today is Valentine's Day, and Leo and I are going to do something that we rarely do—we are going out to dinner at a nice restaurant. It is the year of our 25th anniversary, so I figured we could afford it. I'm looking forward to it. I well remember the first Valentine's Day we celebrated. Leo was still living in his apartment and I went there to pick him up. I think I had some flowers and a card. He gave me a card that said, "I hope that someday you are as much in love with me as I am with you." Emotionally, I was conflicted. I knew that Leo was the best thing that had ever happened to me, and yet I was so commitment phobic. It was an approach-avoidance emotional stance. I also gave Leo a dozen roses on Saturday, and they are still doing well. Yes, I bought them a few days earlier for $10 because if I bought them today, the price would be close to $50. Why waste money?

February 14, 2006

Leo and I went to a nice restaurant last evening and had a nice meal. We ordered a drink, and when we got it, Leo asked, "Well, are you still?" I didn't know what he meant, and then he told me that he wanted to know if I was still in love with him now as he was then. I told him, "Yes!"

February 15, 2006

It has been a comfort to me to hear of Leo telling our friends that our trip to Ireland was wonderful and that he had a good time. I wasn't sure he did. While I tried to keep my "money obsession" in check, I know it raised its head several times. The money exchange was not in our favor; I never knew exactly how many dollars were really being charged when the costs were in Euros, and we seemed to be buying things relatively often. Leo knew (and I admit it) that at restaurants, I would look to the right of the menu, figure what was the least expensive price of things, and then see if there was something in that price range I liked. Leo, on the other hand, was on vacation and ordered what he thought sounded good.

September 26, 2006

The vows that we will say for our 25th anniversary liturgy next Sunday will be the same ones that we said years ago except for changing "15" to "25."

Leo, when I first met you twenty-five years ago, I never believed that I would find someone who would care for me and love me and with whom I could share my life. You know everything about me and love me still. Because of your gentleness, kindness, loyalty, and unconditional love for me, I have learned to love without guilt, and my sexuality and spirituality are far more integrated into my personality. Because of you, Leo, I am alive today. For all eternity, I will be grateful to God for the gift of you—pure grace in my life.

Today, Leo, I renew my commitment to you and to our relationship. I will be with you in the good years and the difficult ones. I will continue to love and care for you in this life to the best of my ability, and I look forward to spending eternity with you and with God. I love you, Leo.

Joe, as I stand here today, I am still in awe at the goodness of our relationship. I prayed that I would one day find someone to share my life with, and you are that answered prayer. This day, I renew my promise to be with you totally and I pray that we will be together always in this life and beyond. I promise to be there for you in body, mind, and spirit; in good and bad times. I want you and everyone present to know I love you with all my heart. May God continue to bless us always.

November 7, 2006

I think of our big 15th-anniversary celebration and even our small 25th-anniversary weekend. People were truly moved by the power of our witness to the goodness of gay unions and lives. What I consider normal and authentic behavior, some people consider courageous and a genuine witness.

November 14, 2006

I am called to compromise my wishes and desires at times because of my relationship with Leo. I'm sure Leo does also. I believe that one of the reasons our relationship has lasted 25 years is because we have both put the relationship before everything else. It has a life of its own, and our job is to nourish it and make sure it flourishes.

December 27, 2006

With Leo, I have experienced the desire to give myself to him physically, emotionally, mentally, and spiritually. With God, I have experienced the same thing. Being human, however, I don't do either perfectly.

August 19, 2007

I opened the blinds to let the sunlight in, and there, near the fish pond in the Abbey of Gethsemani's inner courtyard, sits Leo, listening to the wind. I looked at him and loved him.

November 17, 2007

I will only become holy as a gay man. As long as Leo is in my life and I am in his, I can only become holy as a gay man in relationship with him. To be in relationship with Leo also means that I am in relationship with God. My relationship with God transcends my relationship with Leo in one sense because the former forms the foundation of my life. In another sense, however, my relationship with God is intimately involved and enriched in my relationship with Leo.

Help me, dear God,
to live my vocation with dignity and grace,
and keep me always reaching out to you.
For all eternity, I want to be with you and with Leo.
Amen!

February 6, 2008

Last night, Leo and I were intimate, the first time in about a month. I am going to be 60 this year (hard to believe!), and my "need" is much less than years ago. Anyway, afterwards, we just held each other and both of us said, "I love you."

We are so lucky to have each other. Yes, I know it isn't luck but the result of prayer and therapy. If I hadn't gone into therapy, I don't think I would have been able to allow Leo in emotionally. My commitment phobia would have rejected him because he was so intense at the beginning. Without therapy, I would have probably not stayed around with all the money problems we have had in the past. I'm so glad I did!

Without prayer, I would not have turned to God to help me accept myself and to accept Leo. Without prayer, I probably would have not been able to allow God to <u>seduce</u> me through Leo and with Leo. Without prayer, I would not have developed the spirituality I value and the relationship with God that moves me.

How poor my life would be without Leo. How poor my life would be without God!

February 29, 2008

What has helped me to accept that I am accepted? I believe it is, to a large extent, because I have been and am loved by Leo, my partner in life. I have given Leo the gift of myself—naked and vulnerable—and he has done the same thing for me. One aspect of my "giving myself" to Leo is my allowing his children and grandchildren into my life. My life would be easier and less financially restrictive without them, but they are a part of his life and therefore a part of mine. And I am aware that God is the third partner in our relationship; God is the glue.

March 19, 2010

I remember the night that I committed my life to Leo. I told God that I was scared to death to say my "yes" to Leo but that I was not going to let this man out of my life. I said my "yes" even though this was condemned by the Church, which said that this relationship was intrinsically evil. I said "yes" even though my family would not accept Leo for many years. I said "yes" even though society would do anything to make a gay relationship difficult (such as the couple cannot share Social Security and need special legal papers to have power of attorney in health decisions). I said "yes" even though, in those early years, the gay community did not give much support for monogamous relationships. I said "yes," and Leo and I just celebrated 29 years together.

December 8, 2010

While I lay with Leo, I thought of the vocation of the monk and its holiness and I also thought about the holiness of my vocation—to be a gay Catholic man in relationship with Leo and with God within the institutional Church. I believe that my living of this life is cooperating with God in bringing about change in the Church. I live it as a prophet, not being absolutely sure I am correct in my insight and understanding, although I think I am. And the wonderful thing is this: Even if I am incorrect in living this life, God loves me anyhow and will bring me to himself. All I have to do is to continue to trust his love for me—of this I am sure.

February 2, 2011

This past Friday, we had two couples over for dinner. One was a gay couple; the other was a straight couple. Both couples are friends of each other. We all had a good time. The straight man asked me if I remembered a conversation I had with him and his wife many years ago about being gay and Catholic. I did not, but he remembered it and talked about it. It was an important conversation for him as I talked about my life.

One of the gay men talked about how he "protected his inner child" with the exercise I facilitated at a gay men's retreat many years ago. His partner, who is an artist, had brought a few more sketches of "cross images" for me to consider, and we talked about these.

After everyone left, I cleaned up the dishes and then joined Leo. We held hands as we often do when we are in the love recliner, watching TV. I looked at Leo and said, "Leo, what happened tonight is something that I could never pull off on my own. Without you, it just would not have happened." He smiled because he knows it is the truth.

I was at peace especially when I realize that we have been together 30 years this coming November. When I think about our early years, when I had such a commitment phobia, I cringe. Emotionally, I kept Leo at a distance because I didn't trust that this relationship was going to work. He felt the distance but didn't leave me. He gave me the time I needed to allow him into my life. I am so glad I did!

Oh God, thank you for this man in my life.
For all eternity I want to be with you and with Leo.

August 8, 2011

1. St. Thérèse was a French Carmelite nun. In 1897, she died in her mid-twenties of tuberculosis and was canonized 28 years later. Her "little way" of sanctity was to do ordinary deeds with love and little fanfare. Describing her good works as "strewing flowers," she once said, "After my death I will let fall a shower of roses. I will spend my heaven in doing good upon earth."

2. The Rosary is a Catholic devotion using a string of beads to count a fixed number of prayers. In the Middle Ages, the rosary became a popular alternative to the elaborate monastic prayers prayed in Latin.

3. This is the Post Office where Leo worked as a retail clerk.

4. According to Catholic moral theology, the fundamental option is the defining decision that a person makes to be for or against God. Although I made my decision *for God*, the Church does not accept my expression of faith.

5. St. Bart is a Caribbean island in the French West Indies.

6

ALWAYS THERE IS GOD

Always there is God throughout my life—before me and behind me and at my side and within me.
I cannot exist without the presence of my Father.
June 26, 1990

Father,
I am moving, changing, traveling
on a pathless road to I don't know where.
I am afraid, but in the end, let it please lead to you and to life.
Amen.

August 20, 1971

Religion was becoming a horror story to me instead of a comfort. I had grown up feeling rather proud of myself because I had kept all the rules—I was "pure." Now, I masturbated and could no longer boast, not even to myself, about my obedience to the Church. To make matters worse, I was involved in a sin—one both the Church and society condemned—homosexual activity. To live with myself, I began to put distance between myself and God. I didn't think that he would want anything to do with me, either. Nobody else did.

Almost despite myself, I still prayed and went to Mass. However, my frustration, the unresolved tension I felt, began to change into anger. I can remember going to Mass one Saturday morning and sitting in the back of the church. While Mass went on, I cursed God, calling him every name I could think of to insult him, to deride him, to express hatred towards him. And yet, I couldn't stay content with those feelings for too long.

Somewhere inside, I trusted God to see me though all of this; somewhere, something told me that he had to be of mercy and love or he was nothing. My prayer that year became very simple, and I murmured it any time I thought about it:

Dear God, don't lose me (please).

Unpublished Autobiography

101

In the late '60s and early '70s, I went to confession after every homosexual act because I felt such activity was a sin. I still believed that such acts were wrong, if only for the reason that I had "used" someone else. Naturally, my act of sex was not the deepest form of expression it could have been; naturally, in some cases it was not really mutual, emotionally or physically. How could it be? I had refused to acknowledge that act as part of me; I had refused to integrate it into my personality, and because of that, it was usually just a sexual act that made me feel empty and lonely.

On the one hand, I berated myself for just having sexual activity with no feelings, and on the other hand, I could not seem to integrate it because it was homosexual and not acceptable—not only unacceptable, but also intolerable. What a bind I was in, and I could see no way out except the way I had been trying—to become "straight."

In October of 1971, the bind was tight and I was feeling depressed. One of the ways I handled these feelings was to go off to the woods to get away from it all. One place where there were lots of woods and also where my homosexual feelings did not bother me was at the Abbey of Gethsemani. I went over the weekend of October 23rd for a private retreat. While there, I thought about my feelings and what I was doing about them.

Unpublished Autobiography

Each time I participate in the Eucharist, I see what I believe in—the unity of all men, of all nature in Christ. On the paten at the Offertory,[1] I offer all of my being, offer myself as much as I'm able, along with all the people dear to me—my parents, all my relatives and friends, all my acquaintances, all my enemies. This morning, with more awareness than before, I offered my job, my boss, the people I try to help, my hang-ups, my psychological quirks, my car—all those things that make up my life.

In the same turn, I placed and mixed in the chalice my fears, my despair, my tears, my joys, my trying to work things out. I not only offer bread and wine to the Father, but these realities for which the bread and wine are symbols. I believed this before, but this morning the awareness went further. After the consecration, as the priest lifted up the Body and Blood[2] for all the people, I could not help but believe and be aware that the Father had transformed all my intentions, my job, my fears, my joys, my tears, my hang-ups into his son's Body and Blood, into life for me.

Then as I partake of the Body and Blood, I am really partaking of all that I offered. I am saying "yes" to them, eating them, making them a part of my being. By participating in the Eucharist, I unite myself, with deeper intensity, deeper awareness, with all men, all things, all beings, with God himself, in, through, and with the God-Man.[3] This is all very frightening because, by participating in the Eucharist, I am saying "yes" to dealing with my problems, with my job, with those people depending upon me—I am saying "yes" to giving them all my fullest.

October 23, 1971

Father, it's so simple to put you in my system
with a little theology here and a little philosophy there. But you don't fit.
I don't know what I believe—I feel like one lost in a forest,
seeking to go down any path for safety, for certain knowledge.
Father, show me—blow my structures, if you must,
but please lead me to you, to others, to myself,
where you and others and I are one.
Make me a saint.

December 22, 1971

Father-God,
Who am I and where am I going?
I am in a morality void. Maybe I'm not really Christian.
Maybe I don't really believe in Christ or want to.
Don't lose me, God, and don't let me lose you.
I want you wherever you are. I want me whoever I am.

March 1, 1973

I had it in my mind that somehow I had to be heterosexual before I could do anything about the rest of my life. So, for my vacation in August of 1973, I went to the Abbey of Gethsemani. The question about my life was always there. I couldn't even escape it by coming to the Abbey, where there was no sex, no physical expression of affection or love. I couldn't escape it by coming to this oasis of countryside in a desert of concrete and asphalt. No, I carried my homosexual feelings everywhere. That was the bind I still held myself in. No matter what I did or where I went or with whom I talked, I always came back to my homosexuality all over again. The vacation ended, but not my tug-of-war.

Unpublished Autobiography

I took another major step toward "coming home" to myself. In November of 1973, I joined Dignity, an organization of gay Catholics working within the Church, trying to bring about change in its attitude.

These men and women realized that they wanted to integrate their sexuality and their religious beliefs within the Catholic tradition and practices.

Unpublished Autobiography

What a responsibility we have to and for each other—to help to free men from their prisons, whether internal or external, whether physical, social, mental, emotional, spiritual, or financial. How responsible we are for the poor, the sick, the suffering, those in the institutions, those outcasts of the society. We are responsible for improving their conditions and helping to make these individuals more able to live as human beings should live. These are my brothers and sisters; these are a part of the Body of Christ. These are a part of the Eucharist in which I partake. We are the Body of Christ in the world and Jesus lives in us. We must learn to live and love as he did, for we, the Church, are the extension of the Incarnation.

April 11, 1974

God is not standing over our shoulders looking for every sin we commit. No, he is a Father, standing before us, behind us, and in us, loving us and looking for love in return.

April 11, 1974

In June of 1974, there was a Gay Christian Conference in Dayton, Ohio. The lineup of speakers showed that there were going to be some very knowledgeable people—counselors, priests, and gay activists—speaking about homosexuality from psychological, religious, and personal viewpoints. There would be nationally prominent gay leaders speaking about the history of the American gay movement and its activities today. I was still confused and unsettled. It probably would be good for me to go, I thought, but I hesitated because it was another decisive step down the road to accepting homosexuality.

I kept fighting it, and yet all the while, I wanted to accept it and to be happy and at peace. Finally, I decided I had to deal with my homosexuality. I decided to go. This workshop changed my life.

I saw so many different views of homosexuality and homosexual lifestyles that week. For years, I had seen only one, and that was a negative one. Here I saw not only positive viewpoints but also as many different ways of expressing and living this sexuality as there were people at the conference. But I wanted all the answers now, and I was physically tired and the depression began again. So, I decided to do what a priest at the conference suggested to me.

I went to the chapel and hoped no one else would be there. Luckily, I was alone. I walked toward the altar and sat down in the sanctuary, about twenty feet away from the tabernacle.[4] I broke down crying. I cried and really let the tears out. I spoke to my God as openly as I could. I told Jesus, as the priest had suggested, exactly where I was. I told Jesus of my feelings—the joys and fulfillment of being with a man, the pain and torment of not understanding, of not accepting it, the torn scars of wounds received from an erophobic Church and its doctrines.

I told Jesus I could not go back to where I had been but I didn't know where I really was headed. I was afraid. Before I left the chapel, I asked God to bring me home to myself. As a Christian, it was important for me to include God in my struggle. My sexuality and my religion seemed to be at odds for years, and then, at this conference, I saw others who had combined them. They appeared to be coming together for others, and I wanted them to come together for me, too. In prayer, I surrendered again, if only for a few moments, and I placed myself into the hands of my God. Leaving the chapel, I felt calmer, more at peace.

Unpublished Autobiography

I have spent the last hour and a half dancing with myself and expressing my feelings. I have been listening to records. I have read my first issue of *The Homosexual Counseling Journal*, which mentioned Dignity. I feel good, decent, and gay. I broke out in praise and thanksgiving to my God for my being. I am who I am, and it is good.

August 24, 1974

In April of 1976, I became an active member of Dignity. A small group of gay men, about six in number, began a local chapter in Columbus, Ohio. After working with the Dignity national office and with members of a local parish staff, our group had a home and a base from which to work. We soon attracted others and began to meet for Mass, meetings, and simple socialization.

Unpublished Autobiography

Dear Father,
hear the cry of my insides.
Please don't lose me, and don't let me lose myself.
Joe

May 16, 1976

I really am quite contemplative in nature. That is a part of my temperament and personality that I don't get in touch with very often, but I have a notion that it is one of the most beautiful and rich facets of who Joe Gentilini is. As I sit here, I am aware that I am being good to myself, even in my thought patterns. Maybe I need to touch ground with myself, with my reflective, contemplative nature, more often.

I notice, too, that when I am at this "inner monastery," at this peace inside, I am also at a place where prayer becomes more natural, less wordy, more open and alive. Maybe at these times I am most in tune with God, with myself, with all men. It seems so clear in my mind that the monk really is united in a deep way with all mankind even as he lives hidden away in a monastery. At these times, so am I.

June 14, 1976

Today is Father's Day. My feelings are full. I think of the word "Father." It seems so gentle, so strong, so all-encompassing, so humbling. For if I say "Father," I admit to being "son." One seems to entail the other. When I say the word, my mind pictures my arms outstretched upwards, not in humiliation or necessarily great distress, but as a son. My outstretched arms are an expression of love and also a hope for love. In a sense, there is also dependence there somehow, as a child goes to his father.

I think of this in terms of God. God as Father has become an experience of sonship for me. As Father, he is gentle, strong, loyal, and protective. In him, my life is safe. I am truly son, united in some mystical manner, to Christ, the total son. In him I live and breathe and move. I am a part of his Body, his life. All persons everywhere, all matter of any size, shape, or texture, are in that Body. Therefore, I am united to the whole universe, to all men and women. I am brother, and that places a great deal of responsibility on me, on us all. That is frightening at times. Father—merciful, compassionate, and one that I don't have to fear. With God as Father, I can be who I am. I am safe.

June 20, 1976

As I sit here, I know [I think] that I want to have a mystical experience with God. Maybe I shouldn't say that; maybe that is truly ego and pride, but somehow, I want to be on fire, filled up, ecstatic with him and for him.

Am I just full of emotionality, or is there any depth to me? I don't know. If it is truly just emotionality, my God will purify it, for my desire is true, I think. Oh, it is not really very important whether I feel on fire or mystical with God. All that is important is that I am united with my God, this Being I call "Father." All that is important is that my life is imprinted with Christ. But that means the cross, and I'm afraid.

January 23, 1977

I think that this is the first time I ever experienced God saying anything to me. These were the words that I "heard" in my head:

"Joseph, I love you."

January 28, 1977

I feel your presence, Father,
your movements around me and within me.
I feel your presence, Lord, and at the same time,
I feel my helplessness, my vulnerability before you.
I feel like a log jostling and turning on the stream of water,
carrying me places I don't know.
Where are we going, Father? Where are we going?

March 30, 1977

Father,
heal me from the top of my head to my feet,
from my skin to the deepest cell within me.
Possess me, Father, and make me a man who reflects
your forgiveness and compassion.
Help me to forgive those that hurt me, especially during this season of liberation.

Holy Saturday evening, April 10, 1977

Journal Workshop Exercise: Strategy Six

Imagine yourself taking a walk in the woods on a beautiful day. You get deeper and deeper in the woods and begin to ascend. As you do, the trees become more scarce and you see a little house, one door open. You approach the door and you will meet your inner advisor. He will tell you what you need to know. Start writing it.

Joe, you should know that you are loved. I'm not sure you really believe that or even know that you are lovable. Why fight so much? Could you not just accept yourself, accept your lovableness? This would enable you to relax, become less defensive, less protective as you open up. Go on out and know that someday you will find your mate, a person you can love and a person who will also love you as Joe, very deeply. You will become more fulfilled as you get your degree and get into work more satisfying to you. Then, supported by your love, you will be more filled with peace and happiness.

April 16, 1977

Last night at the baths, I was with a guy I've been with before. After sex, we talked and he asked me if I had a spiritual life and if I prayed. He apologized for asking such a personal question. So I told him of my experience of God as "Father," and I spoke of the Eucharist. Afterwards, he thanked me for answering his questions and he remarked he very seldom talks about such things.

May 5, 1977

I am sitting in my room at Gethsemani Abbey, and I hear only the rhythmic markings of the alarm clock. I did not sleep well last night and so got up for Matins at 3:00 a.m. As I sat in the chapel, I thought of the many times I have been at the baths at this hour. At first I thought of the seeming contradiction but then thought: *At these hours I have been at the baths; now I am here at Gethsemani in prayer. All is in God!*

May 28, 1977

Throughout these years of pain, struggle, joy, acceptance, and fulfillment, I have not lost my desire for God, my desire for union with him. I want to be meshed with this Being, interwoven with the very "stuff" of this God. I can't bring it about on my own, but the desire is there. It is not a sentimental emotion that I am experiencing when I say the above. It is a conviction, a yearning that I have deep down.

May 28, 1977

I accept myself, Joe Gentilini, as I am at this moment. I accept my indecision, my unbeliefs, my rootlessness, my body, my spirit, my mind, my homosexuality, my heterosexuality, my inadequacies. I accept my rejection of Christianity at this moment, and I accept the okayness of believing in it again at some future date if I so desire. I am me, and I can grow, change, regress, push forward, change my mind, my lifestyle, or anything else. I am me and I am okay! (sigh)

December 25, 1977

My mind has thought how many Church people, how the official "line" of the Church, all condemn homosexuality and those who express it. What amazes me is their lack of vision and their lack of real belief in the truth of the Incarnation. The body is beautiful, and it was meant to give expression to feelings and thoughts and values. Christians who hate homosexuals so much would like to deny the necessity of using the body to express the inner, spiritual, part of man; they would condemn them into an alienation and isolation so extreme as to be unchristian and inhuman. Some of these thoughts come about because of the different sexual encounters that I have had recently.

I met a man at the baths last night. We talked in his room and I found out that he was a choirmaster and conductor for the Baptist Church. He spoke just superficially of his anger at the Church for its treatment of gay persons. I spoke of mine in more detail. Then he spoke of his in more detail. I could hear the anger in his inflections, in the words he used, in his tone. When he was finished, he told me that he rarely deals with it directly. Instead, he bites his tongue and puts it out of his mind—not a very healthy way of handling it.

Later, as we embraced and talked, he told me that he usually is the one to listen to the anger of others but no one usually listens to him. Then, looking into my face, he said, "Thanks for helping me deal with mine." While we talked, we both spoke of our ideas of God, Christ, the Eucharist, and of Christianity. The encounter with this man was human, very healthy, and sacred to me. When I think of these things, it only increases my resolve to leave the Church.

February 7, 1978

A letter against my anti-Anita Bryant[5] letter of a few days ago appeared in the paper today. I am terribly angry at religion and don't know what to do with these feelings. I am rapidly letting it get me to the point of hatred of God and all things religious.

February 24, 1978

I think I may have succeeded in killing a good bit of my belief in Church. I respond much less internally now on Sundays and at Dignity Masses. Maybe I can keep it painless. Will probably leave it for another system or be very marginal.

March 20, 1978

Father,
don't forget me here.
I need to be touched and comforted.
Can you hear me?

September 16, 1978

Since I made the decision to leave the Church, I have been at a mixed place. For one, I am able to avoid a situation that only inflames my anger. That is good. At the same time, I think I feel a certain void. There is something in me that needs to be filled. I don't think a life with *no* prayer will satisfy, but I am not sure what to put there. Hence, lately I have been praying some. I do not think I can go back to being Catholic again, at least not how I was years ago. I am at the very marginal end, if at all. I want to remain open to something else, should it come.

November 11, 1979

I had avoided going to the Abbey of Gethsemani in Kentucky for a year and a half because I wanted to "kill my faith," but my friend there kept asking why I wasn't coming. So I came for a weekend in Advent but refused to pray that first evening. The next day, I took a walk in the woods where there are bronze statues of the sleeping apostles and Jesus praying in the garden before his arrest and crucifixion. I took my rosary beads out and began to meditate, fingering each bead with the prayer, "My God, my God, why have you forsaken me?"[6]

After a decade of the Rosary, I found myself saying the words, "My God, my God, how have I forsaken you?" I began to weep but stopped and walked back to the Abbey. I spoke to a priest, one of the Trappist monks. God, how good it was for me to be at the Abbey again. I was able to pray, something that I had not been able to do for so long. And yes, I wept, in joy maybe, in relief that I was not lost or out of touch with God.

I suppose some of it was my recognition of how negative I have been for months, how angry, and how that has influenced me in the negative. I became so cynical and sometimes so insensitive to others—I treated them like objects. That is sin in my life. I am very much aware of how selfish I can be. There is a strong tendency toward evil and also a strong pull toward good.

December 20, 1979

I am aware that I am in need of a conversion of heart, a *metanoia*,[7] and I don't know how to get there. I want to be healed, to be integrated; I want to be living a life in which I am fulfilled. Maybe I want an illusion! All I know is that somehow, I want to be with the Life Force and Source of the Universe, to flow with that Being, this God—a God that I have known as Father.

December 30, 1979

When I am participating in the life of the Church, I am most at peace inside. I cannot understand that very well, rationally. I am aware that the Church has very much been involved in my struggle for self-acceptance and its influence has been very negative in so many ways. Why do I stay? Why do I feel okay there? I don't know except to say that when I left, I became cynical and bitter. I guess, too, all my traditions are involved in the rituals and liturgies of the Church. They have helped me to cope with life and they form a handle for me to use in understanding life. I can't give that up easily.

November 10, 1980

It is becoming more and more clear to me that as a "religious" people, we have missed the point of it all. When we dwell on sins, faults, and imperfections, we dwell on self alone; we are myopic. It seems to me that the core message of Christianity is that the Father, the Breath of the Universe, is total love, mercy, and compassion. Jesus Christ became the embodiment of this "Breath," of this Love, and expressed it, felt it, from the "bowels of his soul." We are truly loved by a Being, a Person, who is the source of all life and goodness. We are totally loved. I am totally and completely loved as I am.

June 24, 1983

It's interesting to me that the Mandala[8] that Jung[9] has spoken of, the image of wholeness, is drawn as a circle. The Eucharistic Host is a circle, and the other day, I was trying to think of my images of wholeness and the Eucharistic Host came to mind. Imprinted on the Host as another image or as part of the same one is the cross. These are centering images in my life, images that bring together all of the different parts, facets, unsettled, and finished aspects, together. My life is all grist for the mill as I become one with this Christ, who leads me to the Father.

January 27, 1984

I am yearning for wholeness. (sigh) I wonder if I will ever experience it. I want to be one with myself, my God, and others. That is sainthood to me. I want it, my God, but I have to detach from that because realistically, I can't make that happen. It is up to you, and here I come back to surrender again, as did Jesus on the cross. "Into your hands I commend my spirit."[10]

January 28, 1984

111

I think of being a monk because it is romantic and different and I would be special. More and more, it seems that my spirituality will be very ordinary, that if I am to become holy, it will have to happen in the midst of my life here. Maybe my vocation is a new one in the Church—living in a committed gay relationship. Maybe that is the Church of the future! Sometimes I don't know what is true and real. I will pray, reflect, and live knowing God will work it out as I at least try to be faithful.

October 6, 1984

I am sitting in the Newman Center chapel before the tabernacle, trying to let go after a busy day. I thought of the Eucharist, my drawing card to the Church, and I thought of Jesus and his life. When I partake of his Body in the Eucharist, I can hear him say, "Love others as I have loved you. Become Eucharist for one another. Be willing to lay down your life for another as I did for you."

What a request, and I can't do it. It seems to me that this message is the bottom line, the judgment point in Christianity and in any spirituality. God, how I fail at this. I have hardly begun on this journey. I ask for his mercy for my failings, and I continue to receive. How can I stay away from Life?

October 9, 1984

This past week, I've been in torment: Should I apply for a loan on this condo? Is it worth it? Will it be a mistake? Should I keep looking? Can I afford it? Do I allow myself to complicate my life by settling down? Can I handle depending more on Leo for financial help with the condo? I was so upset that I was having anxiety attacks and not sleeping. One day in the car, I was thinking of some of the above and I was praying aloud. I told God how afraid I was, and I answered myself back aloud in the words of God. What I said back to myself was this:

God: "Joe, have I ever let you down? In all your years of torment and pain, did I ever let you fall through the cracks?"

Me: "No, you didn't."

God: "Then why would you think I will now? Honey, I love you, and I'm not going to let you fall."

I felt comfort and was aware of the word "honey." Leo calls me "honey" at times, but I've never associated that word in relationship with God. And yet, it seems quite okay—it is intimate and warm and tender. I must believe that my God is all of these in relationship with me.

December 27, 1984

Before I accepted my gayness, I was "religious." I followed the rules and felt pretty smug. My demons were under control for a while, but they had their revenge—my Shadow, my unconscious, would not be silenced, and finally, I acted out my gayness. It was compulsive—not a thought-out decision—filled with guilt and anguish.

And yet, what I thought was terrible and sinful and evil was in reality for my good. The Shadow—my Shadow—led me to the center of my soul so that I could come before God as a whole person. My coming to grips with my sexuality in general, and with my homosexuality in particular, allowed me access to my Eros, to my passion, to the fluids which are part of the source of my life! Oh, I fought it, and I fought with a vengeance. I would not submit! I would not integrate my homosexuality because the Church condemned these feelings. The lusts and self-condemnations tyrannized me and made me compulsive.

With much fear and anguish, I finally learned to transcend the "institution" and to search for a God willing to help me face my unconscious and to bring what I found into the light. Christ Jesus stood at the center with me and said "yes" to my core. By affirming me, I was also able to say "yes" to my core. I became more whole and more spiritual. I became true to myself. "The truth shall make you free."[11]

March 2, 1985

I was meditating on the love of God, on my love of him, and I thought how similar our love for God is to human love. To love God, to really love him and he to love us, we must lower our walls of insulation. We have to trust him, to depend upon him, to lead us to peace and not failure. We have to learn to trust him in the dealings of our lives, often walking in totally blind faith. It is frightening. To love God, to accept God's love, also implies that I am a person who has love to give—that I am in some way lovable.

The thought that hit me was how can I love God and accept his love (in a very deep, mystical sense) unless I was willing to take the risks involved in human love, in love with Leo. If I'm so afraid of dependency, of vulnerability in allowing Leo to get close to me, is it somehow ludicrous to really believe I will be able to let God in? For now, in my life, they seem related. God has shown me through other people, in different ways and now through Leo in a more complete way, that I am loved and I am lovable. He has shown me that not only do other people love me but that he, my compassionate God, also cares for me. "Authentic human love is God's love incarnate."[12] I am learning to love and to allow myself to be loved. Is this not what life is about? I think of the Scripture, which says, "How can you claim to love God whom you cannot see if you do not love your neighbor whom you do see?"[13]

March 3, 1985

I sometimes think about being a saint and really living for God, and then I see what I am really made of—when I really look. I am proud and selfish and lustful. How can God ever do anything with this? I don't know, and yet I know that I do want him or her. Will I ever find rest, Lord?

February 12, 1993

I must go deeper in developing a gay spirituality, basing it on my own inner convictions. I have to develop a personal prayer life and learn how to discern spirits so I can hear what God is saying to me in my heart. I have to trust what I hear. This is so true, and yet it is so hard for me to do. If I look at my life, however, I can see God's goodness to me in many ways. This is especially so with Leo in my life. He is God's gift to me, a way of integrating my sexuality into my spirituality. This is God's mercy to me. I'm attracted to his mercy and here it is right there in my life.

May 30, 1993

People don't understand why I come to a monastery for vacation. They see me being friendly, sociable, and lively. They don't see this other dimension. They don't see that basically I am an introvert, that I get charged up by going inside myself. Extroverts get charged up by being social, by connecting with people. I usually don't. Hence, the importance of the monastery for me. It is a place of silence, solitude, and surrender. In this place, I can again connect with myself, accept myself a bit more, touch God hopefully, and return to others with something to share.

January 26, 1994

My task in life is to hold on to the belief that I am a son of God, that I am loved as a son in spite of whatever Church may say about me as gay. Even though all condemn me, I must hold on to the belief that God loves me as I am, as a son, as a gay son. The Father knew that I would be tempted to hate myself, to doubt myself and him, to believe that gay is bad, that I am bad. God wanted me to risk everything—security of following all the rules, security in following the laws of the Church—and realize I truly must stand alone before him and with him (because Christ stands with me) and come to the Father naked and alone. He must have known that this would be the greatest act of faith I could make.

I am who I am before you, my God, and in you I do place my trust.

September 29, 1995

I sat down and rested and then thought of putting Christ in the empty chair[14] before me. I began by saying, "Love me; please love me," and then I closed my eyes. I answered in the words of Christ, "I do love you," but felt nothing. And then I said, "I don't know how to accept it." I began to cry again, and he asked me, "What would you have to give up to accept it?" I shook inside again, and out came the words: "I'd have to give up my security of being sure I am right according to the rules. I'd have to give up my righteousness."

I'll have to be autonomous and adult. I'll have to give up my trying to get the Church's approval and stand on my own two feet, making choices that follow from the truth of my experiences. I'll have to give up demanding to know why gay is, why Joe is gay.

February 18, 1996

I may not ever fully realize the *why* of my being gay, but it may just be coincidental. God allowed it, and it was up to me to grow and develop and use it. It may also be a very definite decision of God's so that this variation of sexuality would grow in the world. I may very well be a part of the active creative thought and will of God to bring forth a new mode of being in the world—gay coupledom—to show the world that while sexuality between a man and a woman is good and can be fruitful with children, sexuality may also be expressed between two persons of the same sex and be fruitful in other ways. It may show the world that God loves everyone with a personal, earthy, jealous, and passionate love and that we will experience this cosmic love for all eternity in the next life.

May 25, 1996

Trust is the main task that I have to work on right now, maybe for my lifetime. I have to trust my own experiences of being gay and Catholic. I have to trust my own experiences of being loved and cared for by Leo and of loving and caring for him. My actions do speak loudly, I think. I also have to learn to trust more this God, this Force of Love, to really believe that he/she loves me beyond my wildest imagination and will never let me down. Haven't I had numerous encounters or "experiences" to know this? What more can I ever want?

July 30, 1996

Father,
I have tried to the best of my ability to deal with my sexual orientation
and with my spirituality.
I could be wrong in accepting it and living it, but I am not sure of that.
I don't know what is right or wrong.
I do know I want you above all else and the thought that
I would not be with you for eternity
scares me, frightens me, panics me.
You are all good and all holy. You know me through and through,
and I offer my entire being to you.
Please love me, have mercy on me, and guide me
on the path you want me to walk.
If the path I am on is delusion, I beg you to come in and change my life.
I can't go back, however, to living the pain and panic before Leo.
I don't think I could survive—in that sense, Father,
you will have to do something dramatic.
I am a weak, sinful human being. You are God! You can do anything.
If I am on the right path, then please remove my doubts, if possible,
but like Jesus, I want whatever you will for me.
I want to trust you as all good. If I ever become a saint,
maybe it will be that ultimately I surrendered to you and trusted you.

Father, into your hands I place myself.
Love me into yourself and forgive me all of my sins, please.

October 9, 1996

While I don't believe I am in any "dark night," there is an uncertainty inside as I try to do something with or [to] free myself from my burdens of guilt and fear, the two demons in my life. Maybe in this sense it is a dark night—an experience of doubt. I've had a period of dark night before that lasted a long time. When it ended, I had learned to accept myself as gay. Then another and I learned to accept myself as gay and Catholic. Who knows where I am going now—where is it all leading?

February 5, 1997

I like to wear leather. I get in touch with a rawness, a sense of power and control. I get in touch with being a top in sexual activity, talking with a sexual rawness in my voice. In a way, I interpret that as a sense of my own masculine power, and yet, I think that masculinity is not defined by being powerful or "over" someone else, and I know that. In fact, in my life with others, I am not powerful and controlling. Maybe that is why it comes out this way.

June 11, 1997

The body is holy, and all of its parts are good. I've noticed the different experiences between sex alone or with Leo. They are different, and frankly, I enjoy both. Masturbation gets me in touch with myself, with my body, and I enjoy that. Sex with Leo is a shared experience, a communication with another person. It involves opening up my emotional self to Leo in a selfless act of intimacy.

October 12, 1997

For me, the Eros/passion of my life was the source of both "passions." The Eros/passion fed my interest in sensuality and it also was the source of my passion in prayer. Then, they were really not integrated. Now, with Leo in my life, I am more integrated. As I write this, I know that I'm still not fully integrated but I think I know I am more integrated than before. God, what will it be like when I'm really integrated? Maybe then I will really "experience" you and me together.

March 24, 1998

I thought briefly about my life and asked God aloud, "What do you want me to do with my life?" I answered myself aloud with some interesting words: "I want you to love yourself." As soon as I said it aloud, my whole body just shook and trembled. It was a wonderful experience. Now, can I make it real? I will try to love myself more, give myself some breaks, and be kind to myself.

March 30, 1998

At dinner with a close friend, we started talking about dancing. I mentioned to my friend about my experience at the dance bar when I do my best praying. Leo was mentioning how he feels almost cosmic while dancing and feels united to everything and everyone. He mentioned also how his sexuality and spirituality are so closely tied together and that it is almost the closest thing he has that connects him with God. My friend agreed.

It was then that I mentioned my mystical experience at work looking at the picture of Leo and the one of Jesus, which are right by each other on my desk. At one point I looked at both of them and something inside said (as if in the voice of Jesus), "When you receive love from Leo or give him love, know that it is I who am also loving you and it is I who am also receiv-

117

ing your love." I also mentioned that in one of my journal entries, I had written that early in my life, I tried to "become holy" by ascetic practices. Later, I only dreamed of living that way as an ideal because I really wasn't able to do it. Now, I realize more that if I become holy, it will include my sensuality or maybe I will even become holy in the midst of and through my sensuality.

We talked really deeply last night, and we all thought how surprised some Religious Right individuals would be that we talked about God and our relationship with him/her while also talking about sexuality. In many ways, we are more integrated than even I sometimes realize.

July 8, 1998

I was looking up at the ceiling over my desk, thinking of Leo and the good that is in my life, and said in a quiet but audible voice, "I guess you (God) really do love me," and I immediately heard in my soul, "With all my heart." I do believe that God does love me.

July 22, 1998

I really have to affirm and reaffirm that I'm doing okay with God and with myself. I have to trust the process that is taking place and truly believe that I am on the right path leading to him. Sometimes I really doubt myself and think I am living in some kind of delusion-land and that my "locu-tions" are just my own imagination or wishful thinking. I am not going to go down that road, however, because it leads nowhere. God knows that I want to love him and be with him, and that is just going to have to be enough.

August 31, 1998

I was reading my journal entries from my last Gethsemani retreat. The music on the CD was the *Agnus Dei*.[15] Something was triggered inside, and I began to pray. I told God that I wanted to love him with all my heart. My body seemed to reach out almost as if there was a small current of elec-tricity flowing through my arms, hands, and torso. My eyes teared up slightly, and I just rested knowing that God loves me. It was almost as if waves of God's love and acceptance permeated my being.

God, I do want you—for all eternity I want to be in ecstasy with you.

October 10, 1998

Help me, Father,
to make sense of my journey and life,
of my contradictions and doubts,
of my falseness and worries.

October 11, 1998

Leo and I went out dancing. I had the intention as I began dancing to see if I could have an intimate experience of Jesus. I tried to imagine that Jesus was in front of me. At first he was above me, and that didn't work, so I had him stand right before me about two feet away. We talked to each other, but I don't remember all that we talked about except this: I told him that I wanted him in my life and wanted to be with him. He looked at me and said, "I want you far more than you could ever want me, and you want me a lot." I tried to just shut up and let those words hit me, to let God's love of "wanting me" reach me inside, but I don't know how successful I was at first.

January 25, 1999

In my mind, while I was dancing, Jesus just kept reaching out to me with his outstretched arms and hands. "Why won't you let me save you, Joe? Why won't you let me love you?" I got teary-eyed and yet slightly frightened and opened my eyes. I had to break that scene because—I don't know why—but I pulled back emotionally.

I then closed my eyes again and got into the dancing for a few minutes. I thought of something sexual and pleasant and thought about staying there, but I decided that while the sexual thoughts were okay, I wanted to go with my image with God.

The image changed again. Jesus was sitting or standing—I don't know—but he took my hands, looked me in the eyes, and said, "Joe, you love me in Leo, but now I want you to love me as I am. I love you just as you are, a gay man. I love you with all your inadequacy feelings, with all your lustfulness, with all the things that you find so difficult to accept. I love you, and I want to be in you."

I found myself saying right back to him, "I want to love you and to trust you. I want to be in you, too." It was such a mutual sharing of our deepest selves, and yet I still resisted at some level. Then I remembered a conversation with my psychologist the first time that I introduced Leo to him in 1982. Leo and I were only in our relationship a few months. He looked at Leo and said, "Leo, there is something that you have to know about Joe. He was raised with conditional love, and when someone tells him that he loves him, Joe wonders what they want out of him. For Joe, love comes with conditions."

I then realized that I needed to pay attention to what was happening. There was an important message here for me and I needed to be aware of it. I thought, *No wonder I resist God: I wonder what he will want and assume that it would be bad. Can't be—God is only good.*

March 11, 1999

My Lent has been comical. The things I decided I would "give up," I did for only several weeks and then, "Oh, why not?" The acts of charity that I said I would do once a week, I've done maybe twice. I say I love God, and then look at me. What a poor showing. However, I am who I am, and I go to God as I am—a poor, weak man—and he loves me anyhow. That is the real Easter—in spite of my crappy efforts, he never stops loving and caring for me.

It was interesting to me at the spa tonight. I was getting dressed and was in front of the mirror. Up to now, I didn't particularly like to look at myself because I get in touch with all of my criticism about myself—my looks, my hyperness, and my inadequacy. Tonight I looked at myself and just said that I loved me as I am with my hyperness and physical looks. I just am, and I accepted me. God, what a difference in me. Thank you, Father.

March 29, 1999

A good friend commented again on how Leo and I are gifts to him in our acceptance of who he is discovering himself to be. His note overwhelmed me, and yet I know, this is goodness here and I know its source— Christ. Christ uses me and Leo—he loves through us. I can't explain what I mean—I don't know how, because it is profound in its simplicity. This is my "priesthood"—there is something in me that allows others to feel accepted, encouraged, and worthwhile—loved. This is there not because I'm so good but because Christ lives in me and I want him here, allow him to be here, and he touches others through and with me. It's not like I don't love others and accept them in my humanity, because I do, but, in a mystical sense, I know Christ is here also and is the source of all goodness.

May 30, 1999

I believe that I am being called to become more emotionally and spiritually intimate with God, to have a deeper relationship of love with him. I do want it, but it will have to grow between us.

June 28, 1999

Father,
you are continuing to shower me with graces and affirmations,
and I am trusting you more and more.
I am also acknowledging your presence in my life more and more.
You are so good to me.
I give you permission to use me as you think is best.
I only ask, if possible, to be clear about what you want,
to give me the courage to do it, and not be overwhelmed by it.
I am afraid of what you might ask of me, and yet,
I do not want to hold back from you either.
I want to give my whole being to you. Come into my life
and be a part of me.
Amen.

November 9, 1999

I haven't quite figured out how to affirm myself, to be humble with the ways God is blessing me and using me, and still not get a swelled head. The only way I've been able to figure it out is to recognize that I couldn't have pulled off all of the good things that are happening to me. I may have cooperated with God's grace, but I could not have pulled this off myself.

December 10, 1999

On the way home from work tonight, I told God that I wanted him to use me in any way he wished, whether that meant that I would only be influential and helpful behind the scenes or "out in front." In one way, it doesn't make that much difference. I want to be with him and I want to be a saint. At one point, I told him that I wanted to be with him with all my heart, and my body tingled. I thought of sexual release and noted that they were somewhat similar but, of course, not the same. I look forward to having that total, all-encompassing reaching out to goodness for all eternity.

April 19, 2000

Today is Mercy Sunday,[16] the devotion of Blessed Faustina, a nun who had conversations with Christ in which he impressed upon her that he is total mercy. I'm glad that I made the celebration today alone. As I was leaving the church, I picked up a copy of *Divine Mercy Messenger*, and it was so conservative. All through it were articles on Fatima,[17] Padre Pio,[18] and a whole section on the existence of hell. As far as I am concerned, they have missed the entire message. God wants us to love him because he is so good, not because he might save us from hell. They publish their articles out of fear instead of out of love.

April 30, 2000

> *God,*
> *you have a hand on me that just won't let go.*
> *I know that I complain a lot and am often negative toward myself,*
> *but I also recognize the grace that is in my life because of you.*
> *Thank you. I also want to thank myself*
> *for listening to the inner self that cried out for wholeness and integration.*
> *Without my cooperation, you would not have been able to help me as much.*

January 17, 2001

While dancing, I imagined standing before God and I was aware that I was holding nothing back. I was just standing there before this Being of total love and was loving him back. I knew I wasn't perfect, or pure, or good, or any of those things, and it didn't matter. I was just myself before God and he loved me as I was. I didn't hold anything back or try to hide anything—he knew it all well anyway. It was not an overly emotional moment—it just was.

April 29, 2001

I believe that gay Christians have an innate sense of the Incarnation— God becoming flesh. Gays celebrate the beauty of the body and our sexuality. There are some persons on the conservative right who would deny us the necessity of using the body to express the inner and spiritual part of being human. They would condemn us into an alienation and isolation so extreme as to be unchristian and inhuman. We can counter that belief with our witness that the body is beautiful and is meant to give expression to our feelings, thoughts, and values. And we only have to go dancing at a gay bar to see that gay persons know how to give witness to this goodness by dancing. We know how to "let go." I also know that many often pray for and sense God's blessings before engaging in sexual activities. We celebrate our physicality.

From the talk *Gay Spirituality*, given at a retreat for Dignity Defenders[19] in Columbus, Ohio

April 29, 2001

At the Abbey of Gethsemani, as I sat in church before Jesus, I found myself hungering to be united with God. I just "was" before him, loving him, being present to him. I do hunger for God in my life—in fact, this is the most important thing in my life. The surprising thing is that the more I hunger, the greater the hunger becomes. Somewhere in this time period, I realized that God also hungers to be with me, that this is not a one-way process. God hungers with an incomprehensible love for contact and relationship with us humans, with me. His hunger for me is even more intense and insistent than my hunger for him. He wants me to be in his life and to be in my life even more than I want to be in his and to have him be in mine. I do want to be one with him. Even as I type this, my eyes fill up with tears.

I do want you, my good, good God.

May 26, 2001

At Communion, I told Jesus that I loved him and reflected on the homily. At one point, I tried to "shut up" and think of Jesus. I "saw" him standing there, and I stood before him. I didn't want to kneel down but to stand up before him. Then he hugged me or I hugged him. It was interesting because I "saw" this in my imagination and yet, at the same time, I "felt" the hug. It was ordinary. I even questioned it myself, and yet this was a different experience than I have had before and I recognized that.

August 22, 2001

At the Abbey of Gethsemani, I went to Lauds and then to the Community Mass. At Mass, those who wish can come up to the front of the church just behind the monks. After Mass, I just stayed there as others left. The lights were dimmed, and I was alone with Jesus in my being and in the Tabernacle just ahead.

Looking at the Tabernacle candle, I was aware that I was part of the Body of Christ. The Eucharist is the heartbeat of the Cosmic Christ at the center of all reality. Jesus was in my being, and I participated in the extension of his Incarnation in the world. We were one. What an awesome reality. I told God to use me as he wished.

I love Leo, and because of Leo's love, I love myself and accept myself. Because I love and accept myself, with all of my contradictions and with my goodness, I can accept and love God, who made me and continues to love me into existence.

I want God and I want Leo.
I love God and I love Leo.
God lives and loves in Leo.
God lives and loves in me.

I will get to heaven because
In loving Leo, I am loving God.
In loving God, I am loving Leo.
In loving either and both of them, I am loving myself.

Fill me up with such a desire for you, my God, that I will spend my life here and my life in eternity expanding this desire. I want you for all eternity in an ecstatic union of love.

October 6, 2001

I would like to reinterpret original sin by saying that the original sin is the tendency in each of us not to believe in and see the goodness of who we are. That is a basic sin.

November 26, 2001

If I say, "I take refuge in God," I can also understand it as "God takes refuge in me." There is a whole different feel and understanding in saying this, and it is powerful to me. It reinforces that notion that while I can take refuge in God, God needs me to make his love and understanding real and tangible for others. God needs me!

January 27, 2002

Living my life as a gay man in relationship while staying in the Church is helping to bring about the development of the gay vocation in the Church. This is my contemplative task in the Church—a very small contribution but very important. God has given this task to me (and many others), and I am conscious of my vocation, although I would never have picked this vocation for myself. I will never live my contemplative life in a monastery, but the grace of the Abbey has helped me to live my contemplative vocation in the world. My spiritual life and my vocation are truly hidden in God.

February 13, 2002

At this stage in my life, I am closer to giving up the pursuit of perfection. I can never be perfect, and I am more accepting of this in myself. I know this because I am calmer inside and I know that God loves me with all his heart, as I am. I also know that I will always have my feelings of inadequacy but working with them is also soul-work and good for me. I do not have to face them all perfectly but be willing to look at them, see their roots, and work with them as I can.

June 21, 2002

I suppose there is "priest" in me because there is a ministry that I provide for others, listening to them, letting them talk out who they are. I am a Christ-bearer in the world. Isn't this what we all are called to be?

August 27, 2002

I am in a different place in my relationship with God. I do experience God as a Being who is so loving and accepting that it is incomprehensible. This God is personal and yet more than anything I could ever conceive or define. I am drawn to this Cosmic God, this lover. He loves me just as I am.

October 30, 2002

I have mused about the sacredness of people—they are also incarnations of God in the world—sacraments—and that is why it is important to respect each person, because in each person, including myself, Christ is present.

November 20, 2002

For the past several months, maybe a bit longer, I have been filled with doubts about the divinity of Jesus. It is disturbing because I thought that all my doubting days were over, and yet here we are again. It seems strange that this Being of Love—God—would send his son to die for us and our sins. It is more plausible to me that God could send his son to teach us how to live. Because of his goodness and integrity, people killed him.

At the same time I say all of this, the whole image of the cross, the death and dying and rising again, seems to be an archetype almost—it is there throughout life for everyone, in a way, although they may not identify it as such. Maybe Jesus was just part of that same archetype and, in fact, lived it out literally in his life. I just don't know.

March 22, 2003

My desire for union with God is the monastic impulse in my life, and there is something solitary about this desire. Every person is, in a very real sense, alone before God. My desire for union with God also includes my relationship with Leo as a gay man. This is my vocation—to give witness to God's love for me as a gay man; to give witness to God's love for me as a gay man in relationship with Leo; to give witness to God's love for gays and lesbians everywhere; to give witness to God's acceptance of us and our sexuality, which only calls us into deeper union with God.

May 30, 2003

Interesting Gospel reading today from Matthew 12:14–21. In it, Isaiah the prophet proclaims of Jesus, "and he will proclaim justice to the Gentiles. He will not contend or cry out, nor will anyone hear his voice in the streets. A bruised reed he will not break, a smoldering wick he will not quench, until he brings justice to victory."

Those persons who struggle to discover and do God's will, those persons who struggle with their faith, those searching for God in all the wrong places, those gays and lesbians who are trying to breathe under the weight of the Church's oppression will be dealt with gently. With even a spark of faith and desire, God will be gentle and careful; he will blow gently on the small flame of the wick so that he will not blow it out. He will gently blow on it to keep it lit. He blows gently with me.

July 17, 2004

It scares me a bit to admit that others see God in my life, even as I see God in my life. This is not my doing but pure grace. And yes, I admit that I am trying to cooperate with this grace. I stay in therapy not because I am sick but because it keeps me honest in my struggle to be whole. My psychologist can look at my journey with a third, objective eye. I stay in contact with my spiritual director not because I am lost and not only because I love her but because she also keeps me honest in my struggle to be transparent before God.

September 4, 2004

The concept of "offering it up" is old spirituality, and yet there is a kernel of truth to it. "Offering it up to God" has power for me, even if I can't do it very often. I believe that it unites my hurt and bruised ego to the sufferings of Christ on the cross. It can transform the hurt into grace, pouring out positive vibes or energy into the universe instead of anger and bitterness.

October 22, 2004

My Lent has been a bust.

I am a weak man, Lord, full of worry and obsessions.
What I can offer you this Lent is just my love, my desire to become one with you,
my yearning for the sweetness of who you are.
I hope that is okay.
Joe

March 7, 2005

At the present time, the Church is unable to see my homosexuality and my intimate relationship with Leo as good, and so I live, at least on this point, on the margins of the Church. At the same time, however, I also live not far from the heart of Jesus.

May 7, 2005

It is almost easier to talk about sex, my wild sexual history, and even my intimate relationship with Leo than about my intimate relationship with God.

September 16, 2005

I thought about my own life and how I live the Lay Cistercian[20] contemplative charism. I do try to spend some time in solitude; I do try to read some Scripture and meditate on it; I do try to do some work, if it only means doing some tasks around the house like loading and unloading the dishwasher, dusting, or taking care of the cars. I do try and be aware of God in my life as I go about my daily activities—to contemplate the mercy and goodness of God all around me and within me. I try, although I don't always succeed, in being open to those around me that come to me for help or a listening ear.

It does seem that others come to me for advice, [for] a listening ear, for some human contact. Maybe this is my ministry—right in front of my nose. I don't have to "do" anything except be open to the persons who come for comfort, to those whom God puts in my life. This flows out of my Lay Cistercian contemplative vocation; it flows out of my relationship with God in the depths of my being.

September 18, 2005

The Jewish people were commanded to accept the stranger in their midst. Today I can think of the strangers in my own life—people who come to me whom I don't really accept, sometimes persons who annoy and irritate me, and people whom I am biased against. And then there is the further, and maybe most important, point: The stranger can also be the parts of myself that I don't accept, that I don't like, that scream their pain to me.

And what parts are these? Well, they change from time to time, but my life has shown them to me. When I didn't accept my gayness for many years—I was a stranger to myself. When I don't accept the fact that my inadequacies are a part of me even when I so wished they were not. My obsession with financial security is another aspect of myself that I don't like. These are some of the strangers in my life that I need to accept and not abuse.

October 22, 2005

Today when I was driving to the store, I thought of all the people I hold in my heart and just let my living and being be my prayer for them. The pain of the world is so extensive, and at least part of my role in life is to hold it and them in prayer. With my rational mind, I say to myself, "Oh, Joe, you can't believe that does any good at all! It is all nonsense." With my "soul" self, I say to myself, "There is more reality here than you can even fathom. Trust your intuition."

In my prayer this morning, I read Isaiah 42:16: "I will lead the blind on their journey; by paths unknown I will guide them. I will turn darkness into light before them, and make crooked ways straight. These things I do for them, and I will not forsake them."

I thought of all the blind alleys my life has taken, and looking back, I see how God was there pulling me forward to himself and out of danger. I walked many a crooked path, and this loving God was *before* me guiding me, *behind* me pushing me, and *all around* me protecting me. Although I often thought that God had abandoned me, he had not forsaken me.

October 23, 2006

There is something prophetic in living my life as a gay man in relationship with Leo *within* the institutional Church. And whether anyone sees it or not, whether the Church approves of it or not any time soon, it is still a vocation that is living in the Church because I am living in the Church and our relationship is living in the Church. This transcends time and place. It is part of the Body of the Cosmic Christ.

December 27, 2006

I am ordinary. I am human. I make mistakes. I love. Sometimes, I don't love as I want. I am not special. All of these are true, with one difference: I am loved, and because of being loved, I am special at least to one other person, to Leo. I am also special to God because I was created to live in love with this Person of total mercy, love, and acceptance.

December 27, 2006

Jesus brings me salvation (another word for wholeness) by loving me as I am, by insisting that I have every right to come before God and expect mercy, and by helping me be the person God created me to be. It takes courage to be the person that God has called me to be and is continually calling me to be.

January 13, 2007

At the core of the universe there is the cross, there is suffering. The resurrection only follows the crucifixion. This suffering is not suffering we "make up," but the cost of living a life of integrity and love.

January 13, 2007

This morning I said my prayers, but sometimes I just shut up and allowed myself to experience the mystical silence of being alone with God in the darkness. Sometimes, I would tell him that I loved him and wanted him; sometimes I would just hold the cosmos in my heart and present it and me before God. I asked God to let me be with him for all eternity.

January 15, 2007

My career was as a vocational counselor for persons with severe and limiting disabilities, and although [it was] very stressful, I did empathize with many of them. Often times, their sufferings were mental, emotional, and physical; mine were mostly emotional and hidden with my feelings of inadequacy, poor self-confidence, rejection, and humiliation. And yet suffering hollowed out a part of my existential being as I reached out to God to help me. My own suffering helped me to have a more understanding and compassionate heart.

February 17, 2007

I try to get up early in the morning while it is still dark. I get the coffee ready, grab the paper outside the front door, and then sit down in the chair that my mom used to love to sit in. Our dog, Kelly, waits until I sit down and then sits by my feet, looking up at me longingly until I give her the signal that it is okay to jump up on my lap. She sits with her back to me as I rub my hands through her coat and then looks back to me as if thanking me for her morning massage. Kelly then lies down and curls up in my lap while I say Morning Prayer and a few others in which I remember all those people in my heart. Afterwards, I just sit softly petting Kelly on my lap and seeing her curled up with her eyes closed in rest.

Kelly is dependent on Leo and me—for feeding her, for taking her out a few times a day, and for holding and loving her. She trusts us not to hurt or abandon her. As she sits in my lap, resting in the security that she is safe, I think of how God takes care of me, of us. I depend on God for my very life. While I'm aware of some incidents over the years when I was conscious of God's protective hand, I'm sure in the next life, I'll see just how completely I was held in his arms. Just as I hold Kelly on my lap and love her, I am aware that the Father holds me, loves me, and is taking care of me and mine.

March 30, 2007

Living a contemplative life is more about "being" than "doing." It is like being a fish in the ocean where the fish lives and breathes, where the fish is surrounded by the ocean. Contemplative living is being aware that one lives and breathes in God. It is being aware that one is completely enfolded and held by the goodness of God, who is loving and looking for love in return.

May 11, 2007

I feel like Moses after he led the Egyptians out of Pharaoh's hands. God led him to see the Promised Land but told him that he was not to go there himself. I believe my witness is to stay within the institution, as I still see that women, married priests, gay priests in relationships, and lay persons called by their communities will facilitate Eucharist in the future. I believe that somehow, my witness to the goodness of God in the lives of gay persons will be diminished if I leave the institutional Church. One of our friends has asked me how I can stay when "Christ is no longer in the Catholic Church." I know that my answer is not really adequate or understandable somehow (even for me sometimes), but I believe my stance is to accept the tension of trying to bridge both the institutional Church and the future Church within my being. I am so aware of the corruption and humanity of the institutional Church, and yet there is divinity there at the same time. I am aware of the humanity within myself with my weaknesses and sins, and yet God is here in my life also. I don't know if I can reject the institutional Church without rejecting part of who I am.

July 24, 2007

God—Divine Love—has taken me with my Italian sensuality and my German perseverance and doggedness, with my gayness, with my understanding of my religious spirituality, and with my tendencies to obsessiveness and compulsiveness. God is drawing me forward to himself and inwardly to my deepest core where I also find him. May God never stop pulling and pushing me deeper into himself/herself.

August 8, 2007

As we search for who we really are, we gradually begin to discover and accept our personalities and the way God calls us to be. I used to think that being holy meant I had to believe and act like one of the Saints of the Church. This often meant being virginal (I lost that one a long time ago), being celibate (I could never quite do that one), or being heterosexually married (I could not do this either). So, I figured I could never become holy and that I would just be lucky even to get into heaven; forget about any sanctity. What I have learned in my life is that everyone is called by God to holiness or sanctity, but in different ways and these will gradually become clearer as we live our lives.

As we allow God to help us know and accept ourselves, we become able to move away from selfishness, pride, fear, or guilt, and hopefully become more loving and generous. The only way that we as GLBT[21] people can become holy is as GLBT persons. The only way we can become intimate with ourselves, others, and God is as GLBT persons. This requires radical honesty and trust.

Honesty requires knowing ourselves with strengths and weaknesses, and realizing that God loves us as a totality. No one is perfect. We all have our own baggage, faults, defense mechanisms, and personality quirks. It is not a question of trying to rid ourselves of these but of giving ourselves to God with all of them. God loves us, regardless. God loves us *as we are*, not as we might like to be or as others, including the Church, want us to be. Everything revolves around our relationship with God. We become holy by discovering the person God made us to be and by accepting and loving this person.

"Becoming Intimate with Ourselves and Sharing This with God and Others," talk given at Dignity/Columbus retreat, October 14, 2007

When I criticize others in my thoughts and words, as I often do when considering Republicans and fundamentalist evangelists, I hurt the Mystical Body of Christ. While I may legitimately disagree with their points of view, when I condemn them with my air of self-righteousness, I put out a negative force into the cosmos, into Christ's Body. When I can hold back my projections about others, I help heal Christ's Body and obviously all of us, including myself. How often I am not aware of this sacred power within my own life!

November 16, 2007

God sees me and loves me as Joe Gentilini—as a gay man. God sees me and loves me as his beloved gay son. God loves me even with my imperfections, my weaknesses, and my constant need for him. Because of this love, I can love myself as I am—a gay man who yearns to love God with all my heart. Can I love myself unconditionally as God loves me? Can I love others unconditionally because God loves me as such and loves others in the same way?

131

Dear Holy Spirit,
fill me up with your grace and love
so that I can clearly reflect your image in me.
Amen.

May 10, 2008

This morning, I thought about all those gay men and women who worry about God's acceptance of them, who are in reparative therapy to change, who don't even think God gives a damn about them, and I stood before God in their name. I am past my "dark night," and within the Body of Christ, I have gotten through my torture and anguish. My life is in the Cosmic Christ, and I hold my gay brothers and lesbian sisters in my heart and prayer.

May 12, 2008

Frankly, I now enjoy being gay. I think gay men can have a very deep bonding with other men, especially nonsexual bonding. There is a *joy* among us in being who God created us to be.

December 8, 2008

Dear God,
help me to live my gay, contemplative, Lay Cistercian vocation
with dignity and grace, always reaching out to you.
Don't ever lose me, please,
for all eternity I want to be with you and with Leo.
Help me to love you both more and more.
Amen.

March 30, 2009

Yesterday was my 61st birthday—hard to believe. I was going to go to Mass yesterday morning, but Leo told me that morning that Quinn, our granddaughter, was playing basketball at 9:30 and that the kids wanted to go to breakfast with us afterwards so they could celebrate my birthday also. At first I said I would just go to Mass and leave right after Communion. On further thought, I decided that it would cut the time too closely, we would be late to Quinn's game, and it was more important that I go with Leo and celebrate with his children than going to Mass. Charity and love come first. Instead, I just said Morning Prayer and thanked God for my life, Leo, and my parents, who loved me into being, along with God.

August 23, 2009

I wonder how many people really realize that we can have a close and intimate relationship with God just as we are—with our weaknesses and wounded humanity.

January 1, 2010

I believe that I am being led by God to be the gay person God intended and to live this profound gay, contemplative, and Lay Cistercian vocation. So couldn't I say that God is teaching me what I need to know directly? Yes, in a sense, but I also believe that I need a spiritual companion to keep me on the path I am to walk, to guide me if I stray, to encourage me to "listen" to what I am hearing in my soul. Even St. Benedict[22] begins his Rule with the word "Listen." And so I try to listen to what I hear in my soul and I have it confirmed or not by sharing what I hear with my confessor and with my spiritual companion, and I accept their guidance.

January 2, 2010

God loves me intensely and has placed his grace, his imprint in me. God loves me because he sees his reflection in my being and I had nothing to do with this; it is and was a gift. And because of this gift, I can love myself, to love whatever it is that God sees in my life. I allow him to see me in my nakedness and in my weaknesses. God also sees me in my gentleness, my faithfulness, and my desire for God. This is "radical grace."

March 19, 2010

As I sat in prayer, I often just told God that I wanted him for all eternity. I also want Leo for all eternity, and there is a connection. We are a threesome. I do not feel a need to disconnect my life with Leo from my life with God.

May 15, 2010

I know that God not only accepts the human body, but that he also desires to live in our very beings, including our bodies. Over these many years, I have asked God to come into my life and to become flesh of my flesh. It is obvious that if I truly believed that my body was evil, I could not pray such a prayer.

March 5, 2011

For years now, my relationship with God has been one of sonship to God's fatherhood. Many of my prayers over these many years have been addressed to God as Father, a relationship of warmth and protection, and not as much to Christ, although this is not totally absent. I have "seen" this as my being a part of the Cosmic Christ, standing before God as Father. Intermixed at times have been my prayers to God as Father-Mother, combining the masculine and feminine of God, and sometimes just as Triune God—Father, Son, and Holy Spirit.

I experience myself as being called a son by God; and not only just a son, but more as a gay son; and not only as just a gay son, but more as a beloved gay son. Out of this relationship I am called to live within the Body of Christ. My place is to be a witness to the hierarchy of the Catholic Church of the goodness of God in my life as a gay son in relationship with Leo. This vocation finds me in the middle of the institutional Church, for there is my witness.

March 14, 2011

I was watching the marriage of Prince William to his wife, Kate. The Bishop of London began his short homily with the following quote from Saint Catherine of Siena. It is a beautiful quote, and I resonated with it. "Be whom God made you to be and you will set the world on fire."

It seems to be what my journey to God and to myself has been about. I struggled to be the person I *thought* God made me to be, and the struggle was painful. Today I can recognize that I have been in a relationship with my partner, Leo, thirty years this coming November. I stand in for all those gay persons who long for a relationship that does not appear to be there for them. I stand in for all those gay persons who have little or no relationship with God because some religious leaders have told them they are an abomination and cut off from God and that their acts of love are intrinsically evil. Leo and I stand before God and declare our relationship of love, knowing that sometime in the future, gay relationships will be honored and marriage will be a reality.

I don't know if any of this will "set the world on fire," but I believe that this is all in the Cosmic Christ and in the Church community, whether or not it will be visible in my lifetime.

May 1, 2011

1. At the Offertory, the gifts of bread and wine are brought to the altar and offered to God.
2. Catholics believe that the bread and wine offered at the Eucharist are transformed into the Body and Blood of Jesus Christ.
3. God-Man refers to the embodiment of God in Jesus Christ.

4. The tabernacle is a secure receptacle, usually made of precious metals, for the bread consecrated at Mass. Its location is a place of honor in the church. A candle is always lit nearby to indicate the presence of Jesus in the form of bread.

5. In 1977, Anita Bryant, a well-known singer and celebrity, worked to repeal an anti-discrimination law for gays and lesbians in Miami-Dade County, Florida, believing such a law encouraged the recruitment of children for a homosexual lifestyle. The law was repealed, and gays and lesbians lost their protection in housing, employment, loans, and public accommodations.

6. Matthew 27:46. Jesus spoke these words while dying on the cross.

7. *Metanoia* is a Greek word meaning a reversal in thinking and feeling. For me, it represents an appeal for the integration of my sexuality and my spirituality.

8. The mandala is a visual meditation bounded by a circle that represents wholeness. Many spiritual traditions make use of it.

9. Carl Jung, the founder of analytical psychology, developed theories of the collective unconscious, archetypes, and synchronicity.

10. Luke 23:46. Jesus spoke these words while dying on the cross.

11. John 8:32

12. William Johnston, *Christian Mysticism Today* (San Francisco: Harper& Row, 1984), p. 74

13. Cf. I John 4:20

14. The "empty chair" technique, used in Gestalt therapy, helps a person become conscious of personal emotions and attitudes. The individual imagines that a significant person is seated in the empty chair and initiates a conversation. In reality, the person in the empty chair represents an unattended part of the individual, and the responses help to reveal internal blockages and to integrate emotions and attitudes. For me, I found it very helpful to have this conversation with Christ.

15. *Agnus Dei* are the first two words in Latin of the Catholic Mass prayer "Lamb of God, who takes away the sins of the world, have mercy on us."

16. Mercy Sunday is celebrated on the first Sunday after Easter. This devotion encourages people to trust Christ's mercy, confess their sins, and receive the Eucharist on this day.

17. Fatima, a shrine in Portugal, became famous in 1917 when three shepherd children reported several appearances of the Blessed Virgin Mary.

18. Padre Pio, a Franciscan priest, grew famous because he bore the wounds of Jesus Christ on his body. He died in 1968 and was canonized in 2002.

19. Defenders, a leather club under the auspices of DignityUSA, celebrates the integration of Christian spirituality and the leather experience.

20. A Lay Cistercian is a person who feels called to follow the Cistercian spiritual tradition and is associated with a particular Cistercian Abbey. Though not a monk, a Lay Cistercian tries to live a rhythm of praying, reading Scripture, meditating, and being of service to others. I am affiliated with the Abbey of Gethsemani in Kentucky.

21. GLBT is an abbreviation meaning gay, lesbian, bisexual, and transgender persons.

22. St. Benedict, considered the founder of Western Monasticism, established a number of monasteries in the fifth century and wrote a Rule of Life based on contemplation, work, and prayer.

7

SPEAKING THE WORDS I MUST

I pray that the Holy Spirit will give the words to write with boldness to the
bishops of the United States
on the mystery of the cross in my life as a gay man in relationship
with God and with Leo—
to give me the courage I need to speak the words I must!
October 30, 2008

[About 15 years ago, one bishop asked me never to publish our correspondence, and I agreed. Therefore, my letters to that bishop are not included here. I have edited some letters to other bishops to protect their identities. Their names are not as important as the message. Among the positive responses, one bishop told me of a gay family member who, with a partner, adopted two children. Other bishops took me to task. These letters are only a fraction of the letters I have sent over many years.]

I had a letter printed in the *National Catholic Reporter* on October 25, 1973. I was really trying to come to grips with my feelings, and yet I wasn't "out" yet.

To the Editor [of the *National Catholic Reporter*]
I have read your October 5 article on *Homosexuality* and I thank you for it. I had no real intention of writing my opinions until I read the short notice on the front page telling me of the hate mail you had received from a short previous article. I felt that it was my duty to write, and I really wanted to.

The article was, I'm sure, a "sign of salvation," a sign of Christian hope to thousands of homosexuals who read it. Christianity is a way of life that can conform itself to many different cultures, traditions, and backgrounds. It is for all men—a giving of love (Christ) from the Father to the world. When are we going to experience this, to open up to others, to open ourselves to these persons whose lifestyle just happens to be different from the majority?

There are many homosexuals who, in their love for each other, shame those who criticize them and would deny them, not only their Christianity, but indeed, their very humanness. Homosexuals are persons like us all who struggle, love, pray, work, and contribute to society.

How can so many use the name of Christ to condemn these people when Christ himself never condemned them? How can so many use the teachings of Christ to condemn these people in such a manner as to violate the very spirit of Christ himself?

I thank you for this article long needed in the Catholic press and I encourage you to continue to print and discuss controversial topics for our awareness and education.

October 26, 1973

After Brian McNaught[1] publicly acknowledged his homosexuality, he lost his job with *The Michigan Catholic* newspaper. I sent a letter to the editor, Ms. Margaret Cronyn, and to John Cardinal Deardon.

Dear John Cardinal Deardon [Archdiocese of Detroit, Michigan]

I have recently become aware that a member of your diocese, Mr. Brian McNaught, has been discriminated against and abused by your paper, *The Michigan Catholic*. What makes this so horrible is that the hierarchy of the Catholic Church in Detroit, of which you are the head, has condoned, approved, and supported this action. Where is your Christianity? Where is your Christian witness of love?

I cannot understand this type of behavior. The Church is the Body of Christ, and as such she is supposed to act as Christ did. Certainly, in this case with Mr. McNaught, she did not. Even if the Church, as she apparently does, sees homosexuality and homosexual lifestyles as morally wrong, why does she also have to continue to refuse to support civil rights for gays? In Detroit and in several other dioceses she has taken an open stand against gay civil rights, against human civil rights.

Homosexuals, just as heterosexuals, did not ask for their specific type of sexual orientation. Regardless of what their God-given nature and psychosexual orientation is, all individuals still deserve human dignity, respect, and freedom. The Church plays a large role in the social structure and she has an important influence on its functioning, be it for good or evil. By her actions, the hierarchical Church and many of her laity contribute to and reinforce the oppression, the suffering, and the anguish of homosexuals, male and female. She forces many individuals to commit emotional suicide and causes untold personal suffering.

By her actions, in cases such as these, the Church increases the loneliness and alienation of gays, which have led to how much pain, how much agony, how many suicides? What is her answer to the physical and mental tortures that have occurred and do occur; what is her answer to the loss of employment and livelihood and to the resulting disruption of families, and the hurt of innocent people? What is your answer, Cardinal, to Brian McNaught, whose reputation you have tried to destroy, whose livelihood you have destroyed, whose life now hurts because of you?

By her behavior, the Church in Detroit, with you as its head, is saying to Brian McNaught and to all homosexuals: "Your feelings are wrong; they are immoral. Do not affirm yourself. Do not see the goodness in yourself. We go along with the society and culture and agree that because you feel as you do, because your feelings are wrong in our eyes, you do not deserve fairness in housing, you do not deserve fairness in employment. No, instead, you deserve discrimination, condemnation, and alienation."

When the Church acts in this way, she distorts, disfigures, and warps the image of Christ in the world. Instead of being a witness of justice, compassion, and love, as was Jesus, she becomes a witness of hypocrisy, of oppression, of horror. When she acts in this way, the Church is acting immorally. If there is sin, it is here!!!

August 12, 1974

As I got more in touch with my feelings of being good, gay, and Catholic, I began to become more assertive about my rights and those of other gay Catholics. I became somewhat militant, a natural result of years of oppression. I began to "come out of the closet" more and more.

September 13, 1974

Dear Bishop,

With an open mind and an open heart, the Church must begin to investigate homosexuality from a sociological, psychological, and anthropological perspective. She must begin to listen to her gay members and to their Christian vision. Doing this, I know that she will also be required to investigate her theology and her morality concerning homosexuality.

Even taking, at the present time, that she views this orientation and expression as wrong, the Church must take a stand for civil rights and justice. She must take a forceful and active stance for the education of people, to stop the myths and ignorance that surrounds this sexuality. Homosexuality does not exist in a vacuum; it is a sexuality of human beings, and when the Church talks about it or refuses to talk about it, she is dealing with the sacredness of the person.

By her refusal to openly investigate new perspectives of homosexuality; by her refusal to lift the guilt that she has placed on the shoulders of millions; by her refusal to support civil and human rights for gays with a strong voice, the Church sins. By her silence, she says, "yes" to the blatant injustice and discrimination perpetuated against her own members in a variety of open and subtle ways.

In the name of Jesus Christ, our brother, I urge you to begin to make some statements for the human and civil rights of gay persons. I urge you to take a strong stand for charity and justice. Instead of being a symbol of division and oppression, the Church is being challenged to be a true witness of the love and justice of God.

Let us pray for each other and let us pray for the Church that she may begin to be a true witness of Jesus Christ.

September 20, 1974

Dear Representative Edwards [Chairman, House of Representatives Judiciary Subcommittee],

I support House Bill H.R. 5452. This bill, if passed into law, would make it illegal in the U.S. to discriminate against a homosexual person simply because of

his or her affectional or sexual preference. As a vocational rehabilitation counselor, I see many persons, some of whom are gay. I have heard and witnessed
enough horror stories—stories of being denied employment, stories of being
fired, stories of having to hide and isolate one's emotional life for fear of employment discrimination.

People, on the whole, react emotionally to this issue instead of rationally. They
continue to believe the various myths and stereotypes of gay people. Taking a small
minority and their behavior, people generalize to the whole gay population.

This nation was founded on freedom, and our *Declaration of Independence*
states that men have the right to "life, liberty, and the pursuit of happiness."
However, it seems to me that gay people, on the whole, are not permitted these
rights. A homosexual person does not need to flaunt who he is to be in danger.
All that needs to be done is for one other person to inform his boss, company, or
agency. Without protection of any law, even a suspicion of being gay is enough
for some persons to lose their employment.

As a counselor, I urge you to support this bill and to help others to better
inform themselves on this issue. Even the American Psychiatric Association and
the American Psychological Association have changed their thinking and are in
favor of changing these restrictive and oppressive laws. As a Catholic, I see this
as my Christian responsibility. I believe in freedom and equal rights for all men,
including this oppressed minority.

I urge you to hold public hearings on this bill, and then to quickly move this
bill from your committee to the floor for a vote. This is a matter of justice. Delay
in your actions only continues the discrimination and the oppression of millions in
this country.

July 28, 1975

Dear Bishop,

I have just returned from Dignity's Second National Convention held in
Boston over the Labor Day weekend. I found it to be a moving and deeply spiritual experience. The workshops and speeches were very good and quite infor-
mative. However, one of the highlights of the weekend was my participation in
the Eucharist. For me, personally, it was deeply moving as I worshipped my God
with my gay brothers and sisters in an atmosphere of acceptance and dignity. The
Spirit of God was evident throughout the weekend.

In this time when the goals and purposes of human sexuality are being
reviewed and investigated by Church theologians, bishops, priests, and laity,
there will be disagreement concerning the morality of homosexuality and homosexual relationships. The Church has changed her stance on issues of morality
throughout the centuries as she listened to the voice of the Spirit. I, for one, must
listen to the Spirit speaking to me in my heart and in my conscience.

However, concerning civil rights and human rights, I cannot understand the
Catholic Church's reluctance in some places and actual opposition in others to support these rights. Surely others in the hierarchy can agree with Bishop Gumbleton
of Detroit as he urges for civil rights and for the end to discrimination even while he
believes the traditional Church view concerning the morality of homosexuality and

homosexual relationships. I pray that the Spirit of us all will guide you and grant you the grace to see a different point of view. I pray that the Spirit will urge you to support civil and human rights for gay persons even while and if you support official Church teaching on the subject.

I love my God. I love my Catholic faith and find meaning in it. But I must also be honest to my God-given sexuality and affirm myself. I am gay and Catholic. God bless you.

September 6, 1975

Dear Bishop,

This is a short note to inform you that although I will not be present in Washington, D.C., on November 16th for the National Day of Reconciliation between Gay Catholics and their Church, I will be observing the fast in my home.

I wish I could share with you the suffering I see and hear inflicted on my brothers and sisters. I wish I could share with you the oppression that I feel. Just this morning I was told of a case last weekend at a local hospital where the parents refused to take their son home because he was homosexual. At least one agency in the city refused to take him for the same reason. I also recently talked to a fellow gay Catholic who had to leave the city of his employment because his company was conducting a "security" check. Simply because he was homosexual, he would not have been able to "pass" it. This man was a professional engineer. Now he is doing work far below his abilities because he cannot find work in his chosen profession elsewhere. He had a good job, but there was no law to protect him and he had to leave.

You and your fellow bishops are going to be in a unique position next week in Washington. Your conference is stating that the American bishops are for justice for all in this bicentennial year. Gay people suffer very real injustice and discrimination. Will we hear your voice?

I urge you to join me in this fast and in prayer for all persons oppressed in our society, especially my gay brothers and sisters. I also urge your prayers for all who oppress others with their actions and attitudes.

While in Washington, you are invited to share in the Liturgy of Reconciliation. Also, you are invited to stop in at a hospitality suite to meet and talk with some of my gay family. May God bless and guide you. Please, pray for me.

November 8, 1975

Dear Bishop,

I read your recent column and noticed your mention of Dignity. I wanted to let you know that I saw it, appreciated it, and think it is good for people to read about it. I am sure many persons in your diocese are homosexuals, who are interested in their rights and privileges within the Church. Indeed, many people probably think that being Catholic and homosexual is a contradiction in terms. Your mention of the group informs people of our existence and gives a hint of our needs. It is a step that I thank you for taking. I am continuing to remember you, and I again ask your prayers for me.

February 9, 1976

To the Editor [of the *National Catholic Reporter*],

"Facts do not constitute a criterion for judging the moral value of human acts," you quoted Italian Jesuit Fr. Roberto Tucci, as he presented the Doctrinal Congregation's Statement on Sexuality and Sexual Ethics. It is a perfect example of the Vatican's refusal to deal with human sexuality in a realistic manner.

As long as the Vatican and certain members of the celibate hierarchy continue to deal with man's sexuality only through the limited biological viewpoint of St. Thomas Aquinas; as long as they continue to ignore current biological, psychological, and anthropological data, and continue to refuse to listen to the experience of human beings living with their sexuality, Church leaders will be out of touch with the lives of millions.

A principle taught for years by Church leaders has been the belief that grace builds on nature. When influential Church leaders refuse to look at that nature in its total context, biologically, psychologically, anthropologically, and sociologically, when Congregation members can still make statements like the above, how can the official Church's vision, her sexual morality, be anything but limiting, limping, and incomplete?

I would like to see the Church Congregations and Commissions become less myopic regarding sex and more concerned with love, the real message of Jesus. I would like to see them spend as much time, energy, and concern with the morality of violence, war, social injustice, and the institutions that perpetuate the unequal distribution of wealth and food throughout the world.

March 5, 1976

To the Editor [of the *National Catholic Reporter*],

It was a satisfying experience to read the reviews of Fr. John McNeill's new book, *The Church and the Homosexual*, in the recent issue of the NCR. After centuries of dealing with homosexuality, and more importantly, with persons who are homosexual only through judgment, condemnation, rejection, and alienation, the Church is beginning to be more honest and to open her eyes.

Fr. McNeill has presented a knowledgeable and theological discussion of this sexuality. I only hope the Church has enough maturity to listen to him and to the experiences of her many gay sons and daughters. She has so much to learn and she has only begun!

October 19, 1976

Telegram to President Jimmy Carter:

Congratulations on granting pardon to draft dodgers of the Vietnam War. Your decision took much courage, but I think it is morally correct. I would urge you to follow your inaugural message of compassion and justice for all by initiating legislation in Congress granting civil rights to all gay Americans. As it stands at this time, law-abiding and tax-paying homosexuals have no protection under the law. Please consider such a step. You have my prayers and my good wishes.

January 21, 1977

To the Editor [of the *National Catholic Reporter*],

I both laughed and cried when I read the NCR article, "Miami Diocese 'Won't Hire Gays' Despite Law." I chuckled because if anthropologists and sociologists are anywhere accurate in their statistics, the Miami diocese, as others, has unknowingly hired gay persons and continues to do so. How many persons, cleric and lay, work for the diocese but are forced to remain silent for fear they will lose their jobs?

And I cried! I grieved for the Church, which again distorted the message of Jesus and caused pain to human beings. I was sad because Church leaders wonder why there is a credibility gap, but at the same time continually refuse to listen to their suffering people.

Church leaders ask support for their programs to defend human life before birth and to protect and upgrade the quality of life after birth. The programs are good and should be supported, but the vision is not complete. Until all persons are free to be who they are in the sight of God, no one is truly free—not the unborn, not the black person, not the aged or infirm. When will Church leaders realize that Jesus offered equality, acceptance, and freedom to all, not just selected groups? When will Church leaders practice what they preach?

February 13, 1977

To the Editor [of *Newsweek*],

I ask God's forgiveness on those who, in their treatment of gay persons, are violating the Gospel's demands for charity and justice. Anita Bryant and her followers know not what they are really doing to their gay brothers and sisters, and that ignorance may well be their only salvation!

June 1, 1977

Letter to the Editor [of *The Columbus Dispatch*],

I want to make a few observations in response to the letter of the Rev. John J. DeYoung in which he explains his opposition to human rights for gay persons.

I agree that freedom cannot exist without moral responsibility. However, I would suggest that one of the most important moral sanctions of Jesus was the integrity and dignity of the human person. Anita Bryant and her followers seem to forget that point when they urge discrimination against gay persons.

Most gay persons would agree that the sanctity of the home is important. Remember, all gay persons are the products of heterosexual families. Allowing an atmosphere where gays would be allowed to live freely would mean fewer gays marrying to hide their orientation, and as a result, fewer divorces and unhappy homes.

Regarding the Rev. DeYoung's comment about the fear of the disintegration of marriage and family life, I would note that the divorce rate is reaching phenomenal proportions, without any help from the gay community.

Concerning the statement that homosexuality has influenced the fall of civilization, I would observe that homosexuals have existed and lived in every society, regardless of whether or not that society condoned it. Ultimately, no civilization lasts forever but to blame it on homosexuality is a naïve, simplistic answer.

I would suggest that DeYoung has met many well-adjusted homosexuals but did not know it. The happy gay person (and there are many) would probably not be coming to see him as a minister. The ones who do come because they have incorporated society's and the Church's hatred and "sick" label.

As an American citizen and as a Christian, I wish we would practice the tenets of our Constitution and the message of Jesus.

June 1977

To the Editor [of *U.S. Catholic*],

U.S. Catholic asks, "Is Our Church Big Enough for Gay Catholics?" I can only answer that we are already here; we are already a part of this community of believers. Open your eyes and see.

As a gay Catholic who has come out to his bishop, family, friends, and work associates, I can only confirm the findings of Brian McNaught, the gay activist whom you interviewed. "Coming out" was a difficult process for me and others, with much fear and pain. At the same time, however, it was a process that involved liberation, joy, and freedom. I became more open, more spontaneous, and more whole. I became more myself because I stopped denying and hiding the person that I am. My relationships are no longer based upon some mask of who I am. I am able to be totally honest with myself, with others, and ultimately with my God.

My relationship with God has deepened and grown through the years. He is intimately involved in my life as a gay man. Dealing with my gayness and coming out was a death-resurrection reality in my life. God's will for me seems to involve my being gay. For whatever reason, I am who I am and I thank him.

August 31, 1980

Dear Ann Landers,

You recently asked your gay readers to let you know if we were glad we were gay or whether we wished we were straight. It is not an easy question to answer, and so your results may be skewed.

The fact is that growing up gay was difficult for me, especially in this society. In that sense, of course I wished I had been born straight. At the same time, I have grown to love my sexuality, to accept it as the way I love. I have been in a monogamous gay relationship for ten years and we have a good life together. We love and care for each other, have many friends, gay and non-gay, and live our lives. Would I choose to be straight now? Of course not! I am who I am before God, and I am glad that he/she has given me this gift with which to love my partner.

March 10, 1992

To the Editor [of the *National Catholic Reporter*],

I have read your article on the Vatican investigation of Fr. Robert Nugent and Sr. Jeannine Gramick and their work with gay and lesbian Catholics. The

Vatican (and Cardinal James Hickey!) is very concerned that Fr. Bob and Sr. Jeannine are teaching unorthodox beliefs. I have attended several of their workshops and have always found them quite orthodox.

The one difference between their workshop content and the Vatican's is this: They also teach mercy, justice, and compassion. Doesn't the Vatican get it? Mercy, justice, and compassion are also orthodox!

July 17, 1994

To the Editor [of a religious paper],

I read your article, "Voting For Officials Who Support Same-Sex Unions" with regret. The official Church teaching leaves gays and lesbians in a no-win situation. They cannot legitimately marry as heterosexuals because that will not change them and will ultimately lead to the breakdown of that marriage with children and spouses hurt. They are condemned if they are promiscuous and that only reinforces the stereotype that many people have of gay persons. And as this article indicated, the Church considers it "moral weakness" if they attempt to form stable and long-lasting relationships. No wonder gays and lesbians don't often find love and mercy in the Catholic Church.

The Catholic Church's teaching on sex, marriage, and family is flawed and based on old psychological and sociological beliefs. It refuses to incorporate new scientific information regarding gays and lesbians. Jesus would respond differently and that is why so many gay persons accept and love Jesus and refuse to accept the teachings of the Church in this area.

April 10, 1996

Dear Bishop,

I have read your homily given at the Cathedral for gays and lesbians and their friends and families. I was deeply touched. It is so hopeful for gays and lesbians and also for the Church. God is good, and his hand is definitely in your witness of his mercy. Thank you from the bottom of my heart.

March 17, 1997

Dear Bishop,

As a gay Catholic man, I want to thank you very much for the new pastoral letter[2] "Always Our Children."[3] While it comes too late for my poor deceased parents who struggled so much to love me as their son and be true to their understanding of the Church's teaching, it will help many parents dealing with this issue today. Please do not change it in any way because of pressure you are receiving. It is clear, concise, and orthodox just the way it is.

October 25, 1997

To the Editor [of a religious paper],

As a Licensed Professional Clinical Counselor and a Catholic Christian, I was saddened to see the advertisement for *My Brother's Keeper*, a Catholic Youth Leaders' Conference on Homosexuality, sponsored by Courage.[4] Courage is one of several organizations that espouse the belief that same-sex orientation can be changed. It is based on old psychological myths, which have been disavowed by the reputable American Psychiatric Association and the American Psychological Association. Courage also bases its techniques on the belief that gay persons should never accept their sexuality as God-given and integrate it into their personality and spirituality. Instead, this conference and others like it will spawn a new cycle of teenage suicides as young gay persons will feel trapped and condemned. To encourage this conference and its misinformation is wrong.

April 13, 1998

Dear Bishop,

I want to thank you for your presence and talk at the DignityUSA conference in Denver, despite the hierarchical climate at this time. That took courage! Thank you also for what you said to all of us—your apology in the name of the Church, your discussion of the pastoral letter "Always Our Children," and your instructive lesson on the primacy of conscience and discernment. They were much appreciated.

I cannot tell you the number of persons in that audience who either had tears in their eyes or tears streaming down their faces. You, a bishop of the Church, had the courage to do what Jesus would do—meet with us, listen to us, talk with us, and recognize our dignity in God. Thank you from the bottom of my heart.

September 18, 1999

Well, one of the bishops answered my letter very quickly. In one way, I detected a different tone than his other letters to me; this one seemed more personal and maybe more genuine. At the same time, my cynicism is aroused and I know that it could be a sham. However, I will take it at face value: He seemed moved and genuine. I do forgive him although I still believe he and the Church are wrong in how they view gays and how they treat us. They have sinned and are sinning against us even if they and some in the Church are blind to that fact or too weak to stop it. My stance is vocal yet not strident. Contemplative and yet active witness to the goodness of gay sexuality and gay spirituality is what I believe I am called to be and do.

March 29, 2000

Received a very interesting response back from one of the bishops with whom I have been writing. It was the most real and personal letter that I have ever received from him. I do believe that my respectful and nonjudgmental letters to him are slowly having an effect. I am convinced that there is power in prayer and in the witness of my life as a gay Catholic man.

October 7, 2000

Dear Dr. Wing and the Governing Board [of the First Community Church, Columbus, Ohio],

I am very aware of the struggle First Community Church (FCC) is going through as it discerns covenant same-sex unions. I wanted to give you a few of my thoughts.

In November 1999, I was privileged to participate in a discussion on how to help FCC become an open and affirming church for gays and lesbians. I listened to the discussion and was then asked for my reactions and suggestions. This is what I told that group and what I would like to tell you today.

The arguments that your opponents use to deny gays and lesbians our rightful place in the Church are numerous. When you confront and answer one of their arguments, they will bring up another one. They are not really looking for a logical answer, because their argument is fundamentally a negative emotional response to homosexuality and homosexuals. No answer will ever satisfy them.

It is important that your gay members continue to speak the truth of their lives, being able to be fully who they are and having their loving relationships blessed by the Church. If more gays live the truth of their lives, grace will follow and change will come, albeit slowly.

I would encourage the governing board to say yes to covenant same-sex unions at FCC. It is the just and right thing to do, and that, in fact, is what makes the decision so crucial. Voting to table the decision will not change the fact that it needs to be done, and it will not ultimately change the final outcome for the members that stay or leave.

In the '60s, the civil rights movement did not begin because attitudes suddenly changed. It came about because the law was changed and only then did attitudes begin to change. If you make the decision to say yes to these covenant same-sex unions, and then ultimately celebrate them, attitudes will change.

Know that you are in my prayers as you make your discernment. God bless you and all the members of your prophetic church. Thank you.

November 3, 2000

To the Editor [of the *National Catholic Reporter*],

While it is nice that the Los Angeles Archdiocese has had a ministry for lesbian and gay Catholics for 15 years, it still refuses to honor our relationships. Last year, the LA bishops provided $300,000 to fight Proposition 22, which supported our relationships. A ministry that accepts us with one hand but fights us with the other is not an honest or supportive ministry.

Members of DignityUSA are lesbian and gay Catholics who are more prophetic and have a greater sense of their dignity and self-worth. We believe that we have a right to form intimate and life-giving relationships that include the human expression of our sexuality. When the Church can truly support us as self-affirming gay and lesbian Catholics, then I will respect their attempt at ministry to us.

February 19, 2001

Dear Cardinal and Bishop,

Both of you have made statements during the last several weeks that have been nothing but slanderous. The current problem of the Catholic Church in the United States is because men have not kept their celibacy, not because they are homosexual. I know, as do you, many gay clergy who are living holy lives. By saying that no gay man should be allowed into the seminary/priesthood, you discount the many men who are already serving the Church.

One problem is that the Church refuses to review its stance on human sexuality in general and homosexuality specifically. It is hard enough for any priest (person) to be holy without adding the additional burden of being called "intrinsically evil."

The bishops of the United States have covered up problems for years and now you want to lay it on the backs of gay men/priests. The problem will never be solved this way. The only way to make a difference is to accept men into the priesthood who are mature sexually and integrated, regardless of their sexual orientation. To do otherwise will only make the problem worse.

I pray for the Church in this crisis every morning in my meditations. Please do not scapegoat gays but look deeper into the structural problems that exist in the priesthood and the Church. God bless.

May 7, 2002

To the Editor [of a religious paper],

I could not help but notice your recent article, "Vatican Prepares Draft Directives Against Admitting Homosexuals As Priests." The article quotes Fr. Andrew Baker saying that homosexuality is a disordered attraction that can "never image God and never contribute to the good of the person or society."

What a condemning statement that totally dismisses the United States bishops' letter, *Always Our Children*, that addresses parents and encourages them to love their gay and lesbian children who are gifts from God. It also dismisses the good that has been done for the Church and society by gay priests, including Fr. Mychal Judge, who was killed at the World Trade Center on September 11, 2001, and the famous writer Henri Nouwen.

There are many persons who are homosexually oriented who image God's love, mercy, and diversity every day to themselves and to society. It is sad that Fr. Baker is blind to the goodness and holiness in our lives because he does not expect to see it there.

October 22, 2002

I truly believe that my cooperation in the paschal mystery of Christ is to be a witness to the bishops and to the Church regarding the truth of my life as a gay man. I am not responsible for changing their minds but only for the witness. I'll let God deal with the results. This frees me inside and helps me not to allow myself to get really angry. For me, anger doesn't do much except to fuck me up. I become burdened with it. I'm not saying that this is always easy for me, but it is how I handle it.

October 30, 2002

I keep thinking about my letters to the bishops. I usually don't ask for anything but for them to listen to my story, my truth, and the goodness that God has put in me. I am respectful, recognizing that they are human beings, flawed as the rest of us, and filled with their own biases and filters. They are bishops in my Church and deserve respect if only for that.

None of this implies or should imply that I agree with their stances and beliefs on homosexuality and a variety of other issues. Being respectful never implies agreement. My letters are no longer angry in the same way as years ago. Being angry with "violent" words only makes me feel better and makes the other defensive. With this type of anger, the other person does not listen to the message. It is better, in my mind, to say my truth, not back down, and keep to "I" sentences—how a teaching or action of the Church affects me—instead of "you" sentences that tend only to blame.

April 25, 2003

To Whom It May Concern [at WCMH-TV—NBC 4]:

I always watch WCMH television for my local and national news and have usually been satisfied with the fairness of the coverage. This is not the case with your recent coverage of the Gay Pride March and Festival. In reality, your coverage was short and basically unfair.

While there were about nine mainline churches in the parade celebrating God's acceptance of and love for gays and lesbians, WCMH did not show one picture of them but instead decided to focus on one of the religious right-wing protesters. While there were many signs of religious support for our community, especially at the Statehouse, WCMH did not even acknowledge their presence. Instead of getting quotes from the supportive pastors (of which there were many), WCMH only quoted one of the religious right-wing protesters. To top if off, you showed a man who was practically naked instead of the thousands of ordinary gay citizens. I expected more from your station.

June 27, 2005

Dear Holy Father Pope Benedict XVI,

I doubt that you will ever see this message, but I send it to you anyhow in the hope that you or someone there will read it. Happy Easter! I do pray for you every morning.

I am a homosexual Catholic man who has been in a holy union with another Catholic man for 25 years. The Vatican refuses to see God in our lives because it will not re-look at the whole issue of human sexuality. It continues to work against the civil and human rights of gays in this country and, in fact, helps to foster misunderstanding and discrimination.

148

The pain and suffering that this causes is difficult to bear, but I have united my suffering to the Cross of Jesus, and there I find my comfort. I am a faithful Catholic and find value in my religion, but this is only because of my personal relationship with God.

April 15, 2006

Dear Bishop,

The United States Catholic Conference of Bishops is now over, and the bishops have approved yet another document concerning gay persons and our moral choices. One of the statements in the document says, "It is important that Church ministers listen to the experiences, needs, and hopes of the person with a homosexual inclination to whom and with whom they minister. Dialogue provides an exchange of information, and also communicates a respect for the innate dignity of other persons and a respect for their consciences."

Unfortunately, the bishops did not consult the very persons who are the subject of the document, and I doubt that many bishops "listen to the experiences, needs, and hopes" of gay persons. I try to do this for you through my letters and journal entries. Hopefully, you are reading and "listening" to this gay person.

I doubt that many gay persons will find *Ministry to Persons with a Homosexual Inclination: Guidelines for Pastoral Care* welcoming or affirming. In spite of its "kinder" language, many gay Catholics will find its understanding of human sexuality, scriptural exegesis, the social sciences, and its conclusions limiting.

As I have told you before, I remember you every day in my prayers and ask for a small remembrance in yours. Together, we come to God as we are, with our strengths and weaknesses. God bless you.

November 18, 2006

Dear Archbishop,

I appreciate your response to my letter outlining my journey to God as a gay Catholic man. More importantly, I was moved that you actually read what I sent to you.

I would only make two comments. One, the moral teaching of the Church on committed gay unions is not based on the "teachings of Christ" but on a misunderstanding of the scriptures that deal with "homosexual acts" and a limited view of natural law. Two, the Church has changed her understanding of other moral issues in her history (e.g. usury, slavery), and someday, not in my lifetime, I expect she will change her teaching on committed gay unions like my own (almost 26 years of faithful love).

I pray for you by name every morning and ask you to please say a prayer for me today. Thank you.

September 5, 2007

Dear Bishop,

I received your kind letter and am glad that you were able to read my previous letter and a few journal entries.

You asked if you could share it with the task force that is working on trying to develop some outreach to gay and lesbian people. My answer is yes, as long as you don't edit my story. I would want them to know how difficult it has been to integrate my sexual orientation into my personality and Catholic spirituality.

I will pray for you and your task force in the days ahead. If I can help in any way, let me know.

September 13, 2007

To the Editor [of Christianity Today]:

I read both articles in this month's edition of Christianity Today and thought, "What change are they talking about?" In your articles, different methods of measurement of change were used and "change" could mean anything from being "chastely celibate," partially heterosexual however slight, a redefining of the words "sexual orientation" to refer to "acts," or a new way of looking at "identity." I read very little about an actual "change in sexual orientation."

As a gay man who was in reparative therapy for 6 years, in the beginning I also believed that I was "really heterosexual but hadn't found it yet." If I had taken one of your surveys after the first year, I would have said I was "changed" because I was redirecting my focus towards heterosexuality and what I believed God wanted in my life. I looked for absolutely anything that I could use to confirm my desired change.

After those 6 years, I learned that whether or not I ever engaged in another homosexual "act," I still had a homosexual orientation. I learned that trying to be celibate with no expression of a core piece of my personality only brought me compulsive promiscuity, a sense of despair, and suicidal thoughts. I ultimately learned that God accepts me as I am—a gay man—and not as society or church would tell me I "should" be.

I now have a new identity. I am a beloved gay son of God who has lived in a faithful gay relationship for 26 years. Jesus came to free me from faith in the "law" and to have only faith in him. I now know peace and deep joy in my life. Thank you, God!

October 22, 2007

After Holy Week,[5] I'll start sending my letter to the bishops, about three a week. I don't know if it will really make much difference in their lives and ultimately in the lives of gay and lesbian Catholics. But, saying this, I also know that I don't have to worry about any results; God is responsible for those. I am just to give witness to God in my life as a gay Catholic in relationship with Leo.

March 15, 2008

To the Editor [of Commonweal magazine]:

While I understand your reasoning in your article, "Marriage California Style," that "When it comes to how a society defines civil marriage, the voices of citizens, not judges, should be decisive," I disagree. In a civil society, every person should be able to enjoy all the privileges of that society on an equal basis and so same-sex couples should be allowed to marry.

Using your reasoning, the laws that upheld interracial marriage would still be in place unless the majority in society overturned them. It was the Supreme Court who decided not too long ago that the right to marry a person, even with a person of another race, was a constitutional right and overturned these anti-quated laws.

Using your reasoning, African-Americans would still be "second-class" citizens, unable to freely vote, and sitting in the back of the bus. It was the Supreme Court who years ago decided that *all* citizens deserved the right to be equal under the law.

Sometimes, the judges have to make decisions that the people are not ready to accept. I believe this is the case with the right to marry for same-sex couples.

June 18, 2008

I sent out my "gay vocation" story to six bishops this month, and today I received a reply from one of them. It is obvious that he actually read my story and saw goodness in my life. His is the first letter I've received back that even mentioned my relationship with Leo and saw goodness there. I chuckled, however, when he suggested that Leo and I "upgrade" our relationship by becoming totally abstinent. At our age, we are becoming more abstinent anyhow, but I would never categorize that as an "upgrade!"

It is interesting that the bishop uses the word "inclination" in talking about our homosexuality. The organization Courage, which he recommends, also uses this word because it allows the bishops to see this issue in terms of *behavior* and temptation. The correct word should be *orientation*. Even in his letter, the bishop encourages us to be sexually abstinent—"just don't have any sexual contact with each other." It is like, "I'm *inclined*" to gossip, so when the "temptation" comes to gossip, I should refrain. Well, having a homosexual *orientation* is dealing with our entire psychosexual being and not just an "inclination."

August 16, 2008

Write the Bishops? Why Bother?
Article printed in *Quarterly Voice*, Vol. 7, No. 2, [2008]; a publication of DignityUSA.

At a DignityUSA national convention in Philadelphia several years ago, Fr. John McNeill told us not to concern ourselves about what the bishops are saying regarding us and our morality. At the DignityUSA convention in Austin, Texas, last summer, Mark Matson, our then president-elect, said, "I personally do not intend to invest any more energy in trying to secure the approval of the bishops." I agree with them and yet—

I began to write some of the US bishops in the mid-1970s after I became a member of DignityUSA. In 1974 I attended a Gay Christian Conference in Dayton, Ohio, after unsuccessfully attempting painful conversion therapy for the previous six years. At that conference, I listened to religious men and women tell me that God loved me as I was and I participated in the Eucharist hearing God's love proclaimed for me as a gay man. It was an overwhelmingly emotional and spiritual experience and I decided to stop conversion therapy and learn to love myself as I was.

Naively, I thought that others would also see the goodness of gay love and embrace me and this reality. In a conversation with a priest I came out to, he told me that while he wanted me to attend the Mass that he was going to celebrate in a few minutes, he would not give me Communion because he could "see" that I was on my way to hell. I refused to go to his Mass and got in touch with my anger at the Church and society.

Shortly thereafter, Brian McNaught was fired from his job at the Detroit diocesan newspaper because he had written an article on the goodness of love, gay or straight. There was a march from the church where Dignity/Detroit met to the Cardinal's offices to proclaim this as injustice and to affirm our goodness. I participated, affirmed myself, and decided that no one deserved this "spiritual abuse." I decided to contact the bishop of my diocese about it.

The bishop did see me in his chancery office and told me that he disagreed with my moral decision and was sorry the conversion therapy had been unsuccessful but admitted that he would not have refused me Communion. When I spoke of God's mercy, the bishop spoke of God's justice. I also believed in God's justice and added that God knew every cell and gene in my body—he had created me gay and certainly would not reject me because of it. With that meeting, I began a relationship with this bishop until he retired many years later.

Over the years, I expanded the number of bishops I wrote to about the need for the Church's support of gay rights. Unfortunately, my letters were filled with anger and self-righteousness and their responses reflected this.

In 1995, a Cistercian-Trappist priest told my partner and me that the pain of living our lives in an unaccepting Church and society was like the blood of the early martyrs and would bring about change in the Church, even though we may not live to see it. I listened and took heart. Sometime later, I heard Bishop Thomas Gumbleton urge us to "write your stories to the bishops." He said that it would make a difference in their lives even if we did not actually "see" any immediate change in their proclamations. I realized that I had never actually "told my story" to these members of the hierarchy; I had just been angry and accusatory.

I began to write various bishops telling them my story. I did not demand anything. I simply told the story of my life as a gay man and the pain I felt at the Church's discrimination. With some I began a dialogue where I was able to suggest how they could more meaningfully support us in the civil and religious arenas.

Surprisingly, their responses to me indicated that they recognized the pain I went through to become integrated as a gay Catholic and some even admitted that they knew that the teachings of the official Church seemed harsh, even while they wanted to be pastoral. At least one even asked if he could share my letter with a task force he was developing to better minister to GLBT Catholics in his diocese. In order to keep these lines of communication open, some did request that I not publish our letters. I agreed to this and therefore will not reveal who they are. Their names are not important.

I truly believe that the contemplative witness to the truth of our lives will change the Church, although this may not happen anytime soon. I believe that living my life as an openly gay Catholic in a 26-year relationship with my partner, Leo, means that this gay vocation is already deposited in the Church and will one day be accepted. So, I agree with Fr. John and Mark; I am not looking for the bishops' approval and my goal is neither to embarrass them or the Church, nor to militantly disagree with Church teaching. My goal is to share my story and let God take care of the results.

This has become my "ministry" and follows from the grace of my baptism. It is not only my right to write the bishops but also my duty. Even Canon Law[6] supports my efforts:

Canon 208: In virtue of their baptism there exists among all the faithful a true equality with regard to dignity and the activity whereby all cooperate in the building up of the Body of Christ.

Canon 211: All Christian faithful have the duty and the right to work so that the divine message of salvation may increasingly reach the whole of humankind in every age and in every land.

Canon 212-2: The Christian faithful are free to make known their needs, especially spiritual ones, and their desires to the pastors of the Church.

Canon 212-3: In accord with the knowledge, competence, and preeminence which they posses, [the Christian faithful] have the right and even at times a duty to manifest to the sacred pastors their opinions on matters which pertain to the good of the Church, and they have a right to make their opinion known to the other Christian faithful, with due regard for the integrity of faith and morals and reverence toward their pastors, and with consideration for the common good and dignity of persons.

The Spirit of God is bringing about important changes in the Church and is using our GLBT community's prophetic witness to assist in this work. I encourage others who feel so moved to consider this "ministry." I offer the following 14-point guide and hope you find it helpful.

Building the Relationship

The goal is to develop a relationship with the bishop, not to send a quick letter and then be done with it. Realize that this will be a long-term communication process. If you can, try to arrange a meeting with your bishop. If not, then write him.

Know your purpose in writing. Is it to influence or is it to vent and blame?

Use "I" statements, not "you" statements. "You" statements usually come across as blaming. This is not what you want to do.

Do not use words that convey intense anger. You may be angry, but try to take out the "blaming" or "accusatory" language. This only puts the other person on the defensive and makes it more difficult to hear your words and messages.

Be vulnerable—you have to share yourself—your thoughts, feelings, and spirituality. Be humble and not arrogant.

Speak for yourself. Do not judge or assign motives or intent. Talk about how Church teachings have hurt *you*.

Whenever you have the opportunity to see the bishop, make sure you introduce yourself again.

Be respectful, if only for the office the bishop holds in the Church, or if you can't respect the office, respect his person.

Other Important Thoughts on Content and Prayer

- Tell your story about being a gay or lesbian Catholic—the pain and the joys. If you are in a relationship, make sure he knows this and what it means in your life.
- Use the bishop's own language and symbolism if you can. For example, cite the Canon Law mentioned above as the reason for your letter or suggest that they make sure copies of "Always Our Children" are sent to all the parishes and Catholic social service agencies in the diocese.
- Deal with one issue in your letter, taking them as they surface instead of trying to deal with all of your issues in one letter.

154

- Even if you find it offensive, make sure you read the diocesan paper. If there is an article on homosexuality or related issues, see if there is a letter you can write to give your point of view. This is another way to communicate.
- Allow God to act—we do not need to be concerned with how the bishops respond or with the results. Let the Spirit use you—this takes an act of faith.
- Finally, and maybe most importantly, pray for the bishop and the Church and let them know that you are keeping them in prayer. You might also ask for their prayers.

November 16, 2008

To the Editor [of the *National Catholic Reporter*],

Your paper reported that the Vatican made "clear its opposition to U.N. homosexuality declaration saying, 'The initiative would promote the dismantling of the human rights system by allowing declarations that are no longer promoting and protecting fundamental rights but about personal choices'." The Vatican clearly knows that homosexuals are discriminated [against] around the world and that our lives are not "personal choices." Our sexual orientation is not a choice, but God-given.

In a similar situation, the bishops of Los Angeles recently wrote a pastoral letter to homosexual Catholics in that diocese stating that the Church's support of Proposition 8 was not meant to diminish their "dignity or membership in the Church," adding that we were "cherished members" and "equal and active members of the Body of Christ." How can we be cherished and equal when we are denied rights that heterosexuals are allowed?

Pope Benedict XVI has written that "homoerotic sexual interactions" are "sterile, both physically and spiritually," adding "that our 'acts' separate us from the very meaning of one's own person in a manner which kills the vitality of self-donative love." Here our acts of love within an intimate and faithful relationship are described as "sterile" and "non-giving." My 27-year gay relationship is not sterile either physically or spiritually, and is very giving.

Finally, a bishop recently wrote me that "the Church is a merciful, compassionate, and understanding mother." How come I don't feel the warmth?

December 11, 2008

While on retreat, I imagined a conversation with God over the ministry I have to write the American Catholic bishops and share my story. Several persons have told me that this is truly a ministry to which God has called me. So I imagined a conversation with God and asked him why he gave me this ministry. This is the answer that I imagined:

I suffered a lot growing up as gay in a society and Church that denigrated my sexual orientation and called me a major sinner. I suffered humiliation and rejection by my own family and by the Catholic school system. Today, I am at peace with who I am as a gay man.

I suffered from the years I spent in conversion or reparative therapy as I did everything the psychologist suggested I do. For a while, I took medication to block any physical ejaculation. I dated women and tried to make "positive associations." I tortured myself trying to make myself someone I was not, and I became suicidal, keeping the means to take my life in my top dresser drawer. Today, I am at peace with who I am as a gay man.

I was promiscuous during many of those years, separating my sexual expressions from any emotional interaction. It was only after I met a man at a gay Christian conference that they came together. Even then, I spent the next 7 years trying to find a relationship without success, and I continued to be fairly promiscuous. Today, I am in an intimate and faithful relationship of almost 29 years with Leo. Many persons coming out of the background I did have not been able to enjoy such a relationship.

During those many years, I tried to find God's will in my life, even to the point of torturing myself in reparative therapy because I believed God wanted me to be heterosexual. For a brief year and a half, I actively tried to kill any faith in a God, at least the Christian God, whom I found so demanding and silent. Today I am at peace with God, a person I have experienced as full of mercy, love, and acceptance. God loves me as the gay person he created.

I have stayed in the institutional Catholic Church even though I see much in the Church which is not reflective of Jesus' radical message of love and acceptance. Because I have experienced the gift of forgiveness from God for myself, I have been able to forgive others who have hurt me. This includes those leaders in my Church who have voiced their view that my sexual orientation is "objectively disordered" and [that] my sexual expressions with my partner, Leo, are "intrinsically evil." Because of this, I am now free to write my story to the bishops, not demanding anything of them. I only ask that they begin listening to my life experiences and those of my gay brothers and lesbian sisters. There is power and humility in such a stance. If I leave the institutional Church, I give up my witness to them of how God has touched my life in relationship with God and with Leo.

Who else would God send? I told God this weekend that I accept his request of me and will be more intentional and disciplined in writing to all the American Catholic bishops more quickly than I have done.

January 31, 2010

Dear Cardinal,

I recently read that in your position as president of the U.S. Conference of Catholic Bishops, you issued a statement saying that New Ways Ministry[7] does not provide "an authentic interpretation of Catholic teaching." As a gay Catholic man, I humbly disagree.

Last year, I sent you a letter detailing my story as a gay Catholic. At one point, I was suicidal. What saved me from death was my contact with DignityUSA and then New Ways Ministry.

On one occasion, I attended a local New Ways Ministry workshop in Columbus, Ohio, and on another occasion, I attended a New Ways Ministry conference in Louisville, Kentucky. During these occasions, I always heard what the Catholic Church teaches on the morality of homosexuality and homosexual relationships.

I deliberately am using the word "relationships" instead of "acts." Courage and similar "ex-gay" programs speak only of "acts" and "same-sex attractions" as if they [are] just some "temptation" that is to be avoided. When we talk about a homosexual orientation, we are talking about a deep and integral part of a person's sexuality and spirituality with the possibility of mature integration.

New Ways Ministry helps gay men and lesbian women, and their parents and loved ones, deal with a profound aspect of human sexuality. The Catholic Church officially does little to help them understand their "discovery" and seems to condemn any organization that fills the obvious void. Your support of Courage does not fill this void because it bases its presentations on outdated and inadequate psychological and theological information.

Without even consulting New Ways Ministry about what they present in their workshops and conferences, you have not even given them the opportunity to correct your misunderstanding. I hope that you can correct this situation.

I pray for you and all American Catholic bishops every morning and ask God to give you whatever grace you need.

February 10, 2010

In my letter-writing campaign, I give a piece of myself to the American Catholic bishops, and I do see a piece of myself in them. I have known the confusion and doubt that God has graced gay persons with his love and care. I struggled for years to find a way to integrate my sexuality with my spirituality, to find a way to see it as I believe God sees it—a variation in sexuality that in no way separates me from the love of God. I believe some of the bishops try to do the same but feel trapped in the Church role. Some have not even begun on the inner journey to reflect on this.

I know that the Spirit of God is working in their lives, in me, and in the Church. Someday, this will all be very clear and obvious. My life now is to be patient and know that the living of my life with integrity is helping to bring this about.

March 19, 2010

Dear Archbishop,

Thank you for your letter. You are correct in saying that there are many persons with a homosexual orientation and that "all unjust discrimination must be avoided." Unfortunately, I believe the Church hierarchy often practices this same "unjust discrimination."

Throughout your letter, you speak of same-sex attraction, tendencies, conditions, and homosexual orientation as if they had the same meaning. As you alluded, the first three of these imply a "temptation" to one narrow aspect of a person's personality, to a specific behavioral act. People who use this language often believe that one can change behavior (acts) in the direction of a heterosexual orientation or, at the very least, not act on these "same-sex attractions."

The more accurate term is a "homosexual orientation," which encompasses the holistic physical and psychosexual aspects of an orientation to love another person of the same sex. This has an important different meaning than same-sex attractions, tendencies, or conditions.

As an Ohio Licensed Professional Clinical Counselor, I know that a fundamental sexual orientation, whether heterosexual or homosexual, cannot be changed. I also know that as long as one insists on the term "same-sex attractions," the holistic view of sexuality is negated in favor of a narrower view of sexuality as only "acts." Because of this, I am not able to affirm the hierarchy-approved ministry of Courage or Church teaching in this matter. Both the Church and Courage use old psychological theories of sexual orientation and incomplete theological and spiritual insights as their basis. I believe that bad psychology cannot foster good theology and spirituality.

As former Jesuit John McNeill has written, "A central Christian teaching based on the indwelling of the Spirit, one that is without doubt of utmost importance especially to those who are gay or lesbian, is the teaching of freedom of conscience. This teaching was expressed in a powerful way in the documents of Vatican II."

Every human has in his or her heart a law written by God. To obey that law is the dignity of the human. According to that law we will be judged. There we are alone with God whose voice echoes in our depths. —The Pastoral Constitution of the Church in the Modern World

As all men and women, I must stand before God, recognizing my own strengths and weaknesses and my need for God's love and mercy. Accepting myself as a gay Catholic man in relationship with God and with my partner, Leo, comes out of my informed conscience and my relationship with God.

It is not only my desire to work for change in the Church's moral stance but [also] my right because of my Baptism. The Spirit of God has touched all of us and speaks to all of us directly, not only through the hierarchy of the Church. When there is an error in Church teaching and an incomplete view of reality, a baptized Catholic must speak out. Even St. Catherine of Siena spoke strongly to the Pope when she recognized that the Pope was in error.

I believe a more holistic and realistic ministerial approach would be to affirm the organization of DignityUSA, which approaches human sexuality in a more complete view while also attempting to assist others to integrate their sexuality and Catholic spirituality.

Thank you for the time you took to respond to me. May God bless you.

August 10, 2010

I can never doubt that God has given me the vocation to be a gay Catholic man in relationship with Leo and with God. God has asked me to live it within the institutional Church, whose leadership denies the possibility of holiness in this way of life. While giving the Church teaching serious review, I listened also to my experiences, [to] my relationship to God, [to] my spiritual and psychological companions, and to my conscience. In that private area in my being, I affirmed myself, truly believing that on the issue of homosexuality, the Church is wrong.

I am to witness to the American Catholic bishops of the goodness of God in my life. It is a hidden vocation, but it seems to be where I am called. I also cannot doubt that God uses me for his good and mine. I obviously don't do this perfectly, but God cares for me anyway. I have asked God to come into my life, to use me as he/she wishes, and to help me to complete the task.

July 27, 2011.

1. Brian McNaught attended the same Gay Christian Conference that I attended in 1975.

2. A pastoral letter, issued by the Church's hierarchy, addresses a specific concern from a Catholic perspective.

3. *Always Our Children*, a pastoral letter issued by the Board of the U.S. Catholic Bishops' Conference in 1997, urges parents to love their gay and lesbian children. Although not fully supportive of gay relationships, the letter tries to be affirming.

4. Courage, the only Vatican-approved ministry to persons with same-sex attraction, has chapters in various cities. It insists that these individuals remain abstinent throughout their lives.

5. Holy Week, immediately preceding Easter, is a time of solemn reflection on the passion and death of Jesus.

6. Canon Law is the codification of the Catholic Church's legal system.

7. New Ways Ministry, an advocacy group that is gay-positive, helps GLBT persons to find peace within their spiritual communities.

IMPORTANT FOR ME
TO WRITE

It is important for me to write an article or something from my journals.
Others need to see that gay persons can be actively gay and holy.
Maybe this will be the direction for my writing. Help me, God!
March 28, 2004

Sometimes I wonder why I have to write so much, but it is important somehow to put my thoughts on paper. When I come here and slow down, I get in touch with the deeper part of me and my insights come forth from my depths.

February 5, 1997

Frankly, Lord, it is up to you to help get these journal entries published.
If you want them, then help me find the contacts
I need and get to the right publisher.
I have been through this with my autobiography, and I am somewhat cynical
and hesitant to try again.
But, as I just typed that sentence, I thought of the scripture passage
where the apostles had been out all night fishing with no catch
and then Jesus came on the scene and they couldn't hold all the fish they caught.
Okay, Jesus, then help me to do this.
I will cooperate, and I am freer than I even was
when I tried to get the book published:
I am totally out and my parents are in heaven.
Maybe Mom and Dad can help me.
Maybe John McNeill can give me some direction.
October 29, 1998

Christ is the heart of the universe, and he continues to draw people and the entire universe closer to his heart, into Love itself. My writing of my life in my journals is part of this force for good, as is my living openly as a gay Catholic man in relationship with Leo. It is my contemplative witness to the goodness of God in my life. Even if I never get anything actually published, my living my life with Leo (our acts of loving each other, sexual and nonsexual) is very much a force of good for the universe. It is all intertwined in the heart of this Cosmic Christ. The Cross of Jesus and the paschal mystery penetrate everything, and my life is a part of this cosmic life of Jesus.

It seems that right now, most of my energies are taken up in actually loving Leo in all of the concrete ways this is shown and lived. And, of course, it includes Leo's actual love for me. We are both in God, loving each other, loving others, and loving God. In my mind, this is truly contemplation of God in action. This relationship with Leo is important, and I know that it is special to both of us, and even to the three of us, namely, God, Leo, and me.

I will spend energy when I retire trying to write this story of my movement toward God as a gay man. Right now, I only have so much energy with work and home. It seems important to me that the energies first go to my relationship with Leo and to God and to my journal writing. I am living my vocation to love as a gay man in relationship, and I believe that this is a force for good that affects the entire Body of Christ. My living this reality is powerful for me and for others. It is helping to bring about the paradigm shift that is coming when gay love and gay spirituality are recognized as another way of communing with each other and with God.

October 20, 2000

I read over this journal to try and catch the spelling mistakes or typos that the spell checker misses and could not help notice the internal dialogue about the possibility of writing another book with my journals. The internal dialogue wouldn't be there if I weren't seriously thinking about it.

October 31, 2000

When I came home tonight, the mail contained 70 copies of the latest issue of *PASSION: Christian Spirituality from a Gay Perspective*. My article "The Oasis in My Desert" was in it, and it looked and read well. This truly is the first time I've been published other than my letters to the editors of the *National Catholic Reporter*, *The Catholic Times*, and *The Columbus Dispatch*. It was nice to see it in print.

Thanks, God.

January 9, 2000

I am going to begin reading my journals and seeing what I can do. It appears that God is going to <u>hound</u> me to at least try and do something with them. Did I say I would do what he wanted or not? I don't think I'll answer this question now, thank you!

August 12, 2004

I do know that God has blessed me greatly, and not just once, but over and over again. These gifts are not just for me but also for others, and I need to give them to others. This may mean by writing some, and I am willing to try if the Holy Spirit will help me.

May 10, 2005

Yesterday, someone asked me why I was writing my story and did I really think anything would come of it. I told him that I ultimately was recording it for myself and maybe a few others. If it went further than that, that would be okay. Well, God, you and I have been here before and nothing has ever happened to give me confidence my story will be told. I am putting my hand out to you, and you can take my story and send it to others or let it rest on my bookcase. At this point, I don't care what you decide.

June 9, 2005

I told God several times during Mass that I loved him. I kept wondering if God really wanted me to publish anything or if I am doing what I am supposed to do in keeping my journals and letting someone else deal with them later. I told God that he had to bring someone into my life to help me edit and synthesize my writing if he wanted it published. I cannot do this on my own! I will try and be more aware of what a priest told me [to do] recently, namely, letting myself savor the goodness that is in my journals.

January 15, 2006

Leo and I received two copies of the book *Sons of the Church: The Witnessing of Gay Catholic Men*. It is not a long book, but both of our stories are in the book. I found it emotional to read. I sure hope it helps others who read the book. As odd as it sounds, I am now more at peace about whether I ever write my story, as our stories are now in print. I feel compelled to write my journals more than I feel compelled to write a separate story. I'll still work on the journals in terms of publishing a "gay spirituality journey," but I feel good that our stories are in print. In my very bones, I believe I am a contemplative and my task is to help others as they come in and out of my life and to offer my life as "contemplative prayer." I am to be in the background instead of the foreground.

March 5, 2006

I have found someone to begin an editing job on my journals, beginning in 1966 through the present. David Schimmel is the editor of *PASSION*, the publication that published my story, "The Oasis in My Desert," in 1999.

June 3, 2007

Somehow, my journals touch others, and I accept this. I don't need to get all prideful about this, but it is obvious that they touch others, and I thank God for allowing me to put in words the movements of the Spirit in my life.

June 3, 2008

I believe that someone reading my journals would see that I have tried to the best of my ability to live my life with some sort of dignity. Oh, there were years of promiscuity and self-hatred, years of saying to hell with God and the Church, but ultimately, God always helped me to stay alive. God always helped lead me to men and women who could love me as I was, who could help me experience their love for me, and who could help me experience that God loves me with an incomprehensible love. God loves me more than I love myself, and he loves me as the gay son he always wanted me to be.

October 31, 2008

I have been praying about these journals for years now and recently have put them in the hands of Father Mychal Judge, the Franciscan who died [on] 9/11. I address him as a saint since I believe he is. He was gay and took care of so many people—the firefighters, gays, and those with HIV and AIDS.

June 21, 2010

St. Mychal Judge,
please take my journals and guide them to publication if this is the will of God.
God has guided me to share them with David Schimmel, who is editing them.
Help me to do whatever you want, dear God.

August 21, 2010

I asked St. Mychal Judge to help me keep my ego out of my journals. Yes, I do want them read in order to help others who struggle with being gay, who struggle with being gay and religious/spiritual, who struggle with non-accepting parents, but I need to step back and let God direct any and all of this. St. Mychal Judge prayed, "Lord, take me where you want me to go; let me meet who you want me to meet; tell me what you want me to say; and keep me out of your way." I need to pray the same prayer!

August 30, 2010

AUTHOR BIOGRAPHY

Joseph Gentilini and his spouse, Leo Radel, were both born in Columbus Ohio; Joe in 1948 and Leo in 1950. Ironically, they both attended the same Catholic elementary school, although they did not know each other then. Joseph always wanted to be in a career that involved helping others. He earned his undergraduate degree in 1970 from the Ohio Dominican College (now University) in social welfare.

Beginning his career as an employee of the State of Ohio, he worked as a vocational rehabilitation counselor, helping persons with severe disabilities to become more independent with the goal of competitive employment. He obtained his master's degree from The Ohio State University in 1974 in counseling and guidance. Joseph worked for another four years and then took an educational leave-of-absence for two years to complete his doctoral coursework in community counseling at Ohio University in Athens Ohio. He returned to work for the state and completed his dissertation at night, finally graduating in 1982 with his PhD. Joseph is an Ohio Licensed Professional Clinical Counselor and a Certified Rehabilitation Counselor. In 2003, Joseph retired from state employment and Leo from the United States Postal Service. Leo was married for twelve years and has three children, all now adults. Joseph and Leo enjoy and love them and their two grandchildren .

Joseph and Leo, who met in 1981 at their parish, maintain their Catholic spirituality and are active members of DignityUSA.

CPSIA information can be obtained at www.ICGtesting.com
Printed in the USA
LVOW13s2232260214

375281LV00002B/390/P